6840398646 1 697

KU-007-736

WITHDRAWN FROM STOCK

The Miracles of Jesus

MICHAEL SYMMONS ROBERTS

The Miracles of Jesus

LION

Copyright © 2006 Michael Symmons Roberts
This edition copyright © 2006 Lion Hudson

The author asserts the moral right
to be identified as the author of this work

A Lion Book
an imprint of
Lion Hudson plc
Mayfield House, 256 Banbury Road,
Oxford OX2 7DH, England
www.lionhudson.com
ISBN 0 7459 5194 5

First edition 2006
10 9 8 7 6 5 4 3 2 1 0

All rights reserved

By arrangement with the BBC. BBC logo © BBC 1996.
The BBC logo is a registered trademark of the British
Broadcasting Corporation and is used under licence.

Acknowledgments
pp. 14, 16, 31, 33, 35–6, 46–7, 48, 58, 59, 60, 61–2, 63, 64,
67, 68, 70, 72, 73, 74–6, 78, 79, 84, 86–8, 94, 98, 100, 101,
105, 107, 110, 111, 112, 113, 119, 120, 121, 122, 123, 126,
133, 153, 154 Scripture quotations taken from the Holy Bible,
New International Version, copyright © 1973, 1978, 1984
International Bible Society. Used by permission of Zondervan
and Hodder & Stoughton Limited. All rights reserved. The 'NIV'
and 'New International Version' trademarks are registered in the
United States Patent and Trademark Office by International Bible
Society. Use of either trademark requires the permission of
International Bible Society. UK trademark number 1448790.

pp. 27–28 Excerpt from *The Dead Sea Scrolls: A New Translation* by
Michael Wise and Martin Abegg, Jr. Copyright © 1996 by Michael Wise,
Martin Abegg, Jr. and Edward Cook.

A catalogue record for this book is available
from the British Library

Typeset in 11/15pt ITC Korinna BT
Printed and bound in Mexico

LEICESTER CITY LIBRARIES	
697	
Bertrams	30.04.06
232.955	£14.99

Contents

Preface

STANLEY SPENCER's pictures of the resurrection are among the most celebrated English paintings of the twentieth century. They are vivid evocations of the dead climbing out of their graves, stretching and blinking in the sunlight. But to some, they seem too parochial. The setting is not only English, but a specific part of southern England – the artist's home village of Cookham.

In bringing the resurrection home, Spencer was following a long tradition in religious art, in which the annunciation, crucifixion or resurrection was set in a particular Italian valley or on a Spanish hillside. And that tradition is built on an inescapable fact. Even if the biblical stories of miracles are held by many to have global, even cosmic, significance, they were still local. Each miracle story is set in a particular place and time.

This book is based on a series of films made by the BBC Religion and Ethics department and, like those films, it is built on recent developments in theology and archaeology. It sets out to bring the miracle stories home, to reconnect them with their true local context and to try to see them through first-century Jewish eyes.

Acknowledgments are due to the BBC production team of Jean Claude Bragard, Anna Cox and David Waters; to theological adviser Dr Mark Goodacre; and to Morag Reeve and Catherine Giddings, the editorial team at Lion.

CHAPTER ONE:

The new Elijah?

The word 'miracle' is common currency these days. It can be applied to showbiz triumphs, medical breakthroughs and bizarre coincidences. You are as likely to encounter it on the sports page of a newspaper as in a religious text. But it wasn't always like that.

'Ere by the spheres time was created, thou / Wast in his mind, who is thy son, and brother, / Whom thou conceiv'st, conceived; yea thou art now / Thy maker's maker, and thy father's mother, / Thou hast light in dark; and shutt'st in little room, / Immensity cloistered in thy dear womb.'

David Hume, the eighteenth-century philosopher who was amazed that anyone could take the miracles of Jesus seriously.

Written in the early seventeenth century by the great English poet John Donne, these lines addressed to Mary the mother of Jesus still fizz with astonishment that the creator of all life should come into the world as one of us, growing inside a young, poor, Middle Eastern refugee.

For Donne, as for numerous poets, artists and believers through the centuries, the nativity is the first in a breathtaking series of miracles that cement and define his Christian faith. But while this string of events – from the virgin birth, through healing the sick and raising the dead, to the resurrection of Jesus himself – has inspired many to praise and poetry, it has left many others cold.

For the eighteenth-century Scottish Philosopher David Hume, the real miracle was that anyone could be irrational enough to believe these ludicrous stories. This 'miracle' causes an apparently intelligent person to 'subvert all the principles of his understanding, and gives him a determination to believe what is most contrary to custom and experience'. For Hume, the rationalist, not only is there no shred of evidence to support the biblical miracles, there is no means of establishing such evidence.

'Though the Being to whom the miracle is ascribed be, in this case, Almighty, it does not, upon that account, become a whit more probable; since it is impossible for us to know the attributes or actions of such a Being, otherwise than from the experience which we have of his productions, in the usual course of nature.'

Battle lines were drawn centuries ago, with the likes of Donne and his fellow believers on one side, and Hume and the sceptics on the other. For many people, it is simply a question of faith. If you believe in a God who created and sustains the universe, then surely that God could raise a dead man to life, or make a sick woman well again. If you don't believe in God, or if the very word 'God' seems nonsensical or archaic, then what could be more implausible than this series of tall tales about conjuring tricks with water and wine, or life and death?

John Donne, the seventeenth-century English poet and clergyman. For Donne, the miracles of Jesus defined his faith.

Today there's a widespread assumption that the only type of question worth asking of Jesus' miracles is whether they really happened. Was Lazarus really dead, or in a coma, or suffering from sleeping sickness? Did Jesus turn up at just

'Annunciation' from John Donne's *Holy Sonnets*

Salvation to all that will is nigh,
That all, which always is all everywhere,
Which cannot sin, and yet all sins must bear,
Which cannot die, yet cannot choose but die,
Lo, faithful Virgin, yields himself to lie
In prison, in thy womb; and though he there
Can take no sin, nor thou give, yet he 'will wear
Taken from thence, flesh, which death's force may try.
Ere by the spheres time was created, thou
Wast in his mind, who is thy son, and brother,
Whom thou conceiv'st, conceived; yea thou art now
Thy maker's maker, and thy father's mother,
Thou hast light in dark; and shutt'st in little room,
Immensity cloistered in thy dear womb.

the right moment, when the patient was coming round, and claim a resurrection? Did he really make a small bread and fish picnic into a feast for five thousand people? Or did sharing his own food inspire the crowd to share theirs?

In the last two hundred years, many scholars have tied themselves in knots trying to find 'rational' explanations for the miracles of Jesus, but the jury is still as divided as ever. One thing is for sure, the miracles were not pure acts of fiction on the part of the gospel writers. Jesus' enemies at the time denounced him for working miracles, and first-century historians documented Jesus as a 'wonder worker'. Clearly, something was going on.

For Christians, Jesus is the Son of God, so of course he could heal the sick with a touch or a word, of course he could walk on water, of course he could feed the hungry. For non-believers, Jesus is no more than a gifted preacher, and the miracles are no more than fanciful hoaxes, or embellished yarns to inspire the faithful. It seems the debate is literally interminable, because neither side can come up with strong enough evidence or arguments to win round the other. But maybe the problem lies more in the question than the answer.

I attended a university debate on miracles when I was an undergraduate student of Philosophy and Theology. It was set up to be irresistibly confrontational. On one side of the table was a scientific materialist and notable God-basher. On the other side was a professor of Philosophy who was a practising Christian. Each was asked to begin by setting out his basic position on miracles, and the Philosopher was asked to speak first. To the surprise of his opponent, and most of the audience, he began with the phrase, 'Miracles don't happen.' After a suitably dramatic pause, he went on, 'They don't just happen in the way that a coincidence might happen. Miracles are deliberate acts of God with specific purpose and meanings.'

In recent years, the ground has begun to shift in the miracles debate. Although there is an emerging consensus that Jesus was known as a healer in his lifetime, academics are now asking a different question of the miracles themselves – not 'did they happen?' but 'what did they mean?' And this new question is driven by an even more important one – 'who was this Jesus?' His influence on world history has been greater than that of any other human being, and his ideas continue to guide the lives of around a third of the world's population, so the question matters to Christians and non-Christians alike.

To try to answer it, decades of theological study and analysis have gone into the words of Jesus as recorded in the gospels – the Sermon on the Mount, the parables, the teaching of his disciples. Until now, that is. The new focus is not on what Jesus said, but on what he did. Perhaps his actions can tell us more about who he was than his words?

The key to unlocking the identity of Jesus lies in understanding the meaning behind his actions. And it is impossible to talk about Jesus' actions without focusing on those astonishing events collectively known as the miracles. So having been regarded for years as an article of faith, beyond the reach of rational examination, the miracles are now right back at the centre of the debate.

The premise for this new academic focus, and for the story told in this book, is that the miracles of Jesus were not just spur-of-the-moment responses to people in need. They may have been inspired by compassion, but that wasn't the whole story. Far from it. New research shows that the miracles were a special language, a series of signs that pointed to the true identity of Jesus. John's Gospel in particular alludes to this, regularly referring to the miracles as 'signs'.

Signs in John's Gospel

Of the four gospel writers, John is the one who most consistently and powerfully refers to Jesus' miracles as 'signs'. Of the miracle in which water is transformed into wine, John writes: 'This, the first of his miraculous signs, Jesus performed at Cana in Galilee. He thus revealed his glory, and his disciples put their faith in him.' And again, as the risen Jesus appears to his disciple Thomas, John writes: 'Jesus did many other miraculous signs in the presence of his disciples, which are not recorded in this book. But these are written that you may believe that Jesus is the Christ, the Son of God, and that by believing you may have life in his name.'

Whereas in Matthew, Mark and Luke's Gospels, the miracles are often seen to signify the imminent coming of the kingdom of God, in John's Gospel they are signs of Jesus' identity. Essentially, what they signify for John is the fact that Jesus is the Son of God.

Although these signs in John's Gospel were set down in order to inspire faith, there was no guaranteed link – even for the disciples – between witnessing a miracle of Jesus, and attaining a powerful faith in him and his ministry. As John writes in chapter two of his Gospel: 'Now while he was in Jerusalem at the Passover Feast, many people saw the miraculous signs he was doing and believed in his name. But Jesus would not entrust himself to them, for he knew all men. He did not need man's testimony about man, for he knew what was in a man'.

(JOHN 2:23–25)

For the people of first-century Palestine, these special signs were far from obscure. Open to the supernatural and steeped in the history of their own people, Jewish witnesses to the miracles had all the equipment and knowledge they needed to pick up the meaning there and then. Jesus' contemporaries saw God's activity everywhere, in births and deaths, in the harvest, the rain, the shifts in the seasons. It was natural for them to

Reconstruction of Jesus raising the widow's son at Nain.

interpret these events as God working in the world around them.

What made Jesus' miracles stand out for the people of his time was not that God had acted in the world, but that God had acted in the world in very particular and significant ways. For twenty-first-century westerners, it is not so easy. To us, the miracles can seem less like a language and more like a code. But it is not an uncrackable code.

By digging into the detail of the gospel accounts, and by discovering more about the mindset of first-century Jews, scholars have been able to decipher these remarkable stories, and shed new light on who Jesus believed he was.

The miracles of Jesus are all recorded in the New Testament, in the gospels of Matthew, Mark, Luke and John. To explore their meaning, we need to examine the detail, taking the accounts of major miracles one by one and trying to see them from a first-century Jewish perspective.

Our investigation begins six miles south-east of Nazareth, in a town called Nein, believed to be the biblical village of Nain. This small community at the foot of Givat ha-Moreh in the Valley of Jezreel was witness to one of Jesus' most dramatic and most telling miracles. The story is recorded by the gospel writer Luke.

Jesus went to a town called Nain, and his disciples and a large crowd went along with him. As he approached the town gate, a dead person was being carried out – the only son of his mother, and she was a widow. And a large crowd from the town was with her. When the Lord saw her, his heart went out to her and he said, "Don't cry."

Then he went up and touched the coffin, and those carrying it stood still. He said "Young man, I say to you, get up!" The dead man sat up and began to talk, and Jesus gave him back to his mother.

They were all filled with awe and praised God. "A great prophet has appeared among us," they said. "God has come to help his people." This news about Jesus spread throughout Judea and the surrounding country.'
LUKE 7:11–17

It's a captivating story – Jesus interrupting a funeral cortège to bring the deceased back to life. It isn't hard to picture the scene: the distraught mother weeping and wailing, supported by friends on either side; the confusion and unease as this stranger Jesus approaches the coffin, telling the mother not to cry; the shock and sheer incredulity of the crowd as the boy sits up in his coffin and talks; the boy himself, blinking in the daylight.

But what are we to make of it? Maybe Jesus really did bring the boy back from the dead. Or perhaps the boy wasn't dead in the first place, merely in a coma. There will never be an answer to satisfy everyone. To those people who saw it happen there was no doubt – Jesus had brought the widow's son back to life. A pretty astonishing thing to witness. No wonder they were 'filled with awe'.

But the triumph of life over death was not what really got the crowd going. If you look closely at the biblical account you find that this miracle reminded them of another miracle that took place a thousand years earlier, performed by one of the holiest men in Jewish history – the prophet Elijah. In fact, it more than reminded them. The symmetry was unmistakable.

The story – as told in the book of Kings – goes that Elijah was staying with a widow in a small town when her son fell ill. The woman – though poor – had been generous in her hospitality to Elijah, so he was distressed to see her son grow worse and worse, and finally stop breathing. The widow was desperate, consumed by grief.

Who was Elijah?

By the time of Jesus, Elijah was one of the two key figures of the Old Testament, along with Moses. Like Moses, he met God on Mount Sinai, and just as Moses came to stand for the Law in the Jewish tradition, Elijah came to stand for the Prophets. Elijah lived in the first half of the ninth century BC, and his life and work are recorded in the biblical book of Kings.

Elijah lived at a time of religious and political upheaval in the northern kingdom of Israel. The great founding king of the Jewish people, King David, had died a century earlier. Now their ruler was King Ahab, who took a foreign princess called Jezebel to be his wife. But Queen Jezebel brought her gods to Israel with her, notably the pagan god Baal.

A statue of the god Baal, dating from the thirteenth century BC.

When she tried to make Baal the only god of Israel, Elijah stepped onto the stage. Elijah's battle with the Queen and her false god was certainly dramatic, ranging from a three-year drought used by Elijah to demonstrate that Baal could not control the elements, to a confrontation between the great prophet and the multiple prophets of Baal, in which the pagan prophets all perished.

After that, Elijah went on the run in fear of his life, but he finally triumphed over Ahab and Jezebel, and over their god Baal. He passed on his mantle to a younger prophet, Elisha, but his place as one of the key figures in Jewish and Christian history was assured.

'She said to Elijah, "What do you have against me, man of God? Did you come to remind me of my sin and kill my son?" "Give me your son," Elijah replied. He took him from her arms, carried him to the upper room where he was staying, and laid him on his bed. Then he cried out to the Lord, "O Lord my God, have you brought tragedy also upon this widow I am staying with, by causing her son to die?" Then he stretched himself out on the boy three times and cried to the Lord, "O Lord my God, let this boy's life return to him!"*

*The Lord heard Elijah's cry, and the boy's life returned to him, and he lived. Elijah picked up the child and carried him down from the room into the house. He gave him back to his mother and said "Look, your son is alive!" Then the woman said to Elijah, "Now I know that you are a man of God and that the word of the Lord from your mouth is the truth."'

1 KINGS 17:18–24

What was a prophet?

The word 'prophet' is now most commonly used to mean someone who predicts the future, but that was not a good job description for an Old Testament prophet. They were fundamentally intermediaries or messengers between God and his people. The messages they brought were often hard to swallow and highly critical of idolatry, sinfulness and injustice. This made the prophets' lives extremely dangerous.

These were wild people, usually men, who lived at the heart of their society but at the margins too. What they had to say put them on the margins. They spoke the unspeakable. Although they did speak about the future – mainly to warn people of the consequences of their actions – their job was more forth-telling than fore-telling. They told kings what they had to do to repair their damaged relationship with God: stop worshipping other gods; stop mistreating and exploiting the poor.

In the Bible, there's no single book that tells us about all the prophets. A major chunk of the Old Testament is devoted to these hugely significant figures. The early prophets, such as Elijah and Elisha, are written about by others, but their followers, such as Hosea, Jeremiah and Isaiah, left us their own writings, often wonderfully poetic, expressing their beliefs.

The similarities between the two miracles are clear: a widow's only son, a premature death, a distraught mother met at the town's gate, a restoration of life by a holy man. Same circumstances, same outcome.

Jesus' miracle, which looks at first glance like a spontaneous act of compassion towards a grieving mother, was at the same time the spitting image of Elijah's miracle. The original Greek phrase at the end of the story, in which Jesus 'gave him back to his mother' is identical with the phrase used of Elijah after his miracle. No wonder the crowds were astonished. Raised on the Jewish scriptures, taught to revere Elijah as the greatest of prophets, everyone who saw or heard about Jesus and the widow of Nain would make the link with Elijah.

According to Luke's Gospel account, one of them even shouts, 'A great prophet has appeared among us.'

But what does it mean, this copycat miracle? If it was more than an outlandish coincidence, if Jesus was acting out a 'sign' in public, then what was the message of the sign? What was he trying to convey by drawing this parallel with Elijah?

To answer that question, the focus has to shift from Jesus, the widow and her son, to the bystanders. Only by understanding the audience can we hope to understand the message they received when Jesus healed the widow's son at Nain. But how is that possible?

There are obvious pitfalls in transplanting a modern sensibility into a resident of Nain two thousand years ago. The way we would react as eyewitnesses is conditioned by our experience, upbringing, education and beliefs. That environment would be radically different for a bystander in first-century Nain.

For centuries, it seemed an impossible pipe dream that scholars might attain a real insight into the minds of these ancient people, and find out what and how they thought. But in the middle of the twentieth century a remarkable discovery offered the hope of doing just that.

FOLLOWING SPREAD:
The Muhraka monastery on Mount Carmel, overlooking Jezreel valley.

17

CHAPTER TWO

The key to the Gospels?

In 1947 at a place called Qumran on the north-west shores of the Dead Sea, a group of Bedouin tribesmen was hunting for a lost goat. Scaling some cliffs, they entered a cave and looked around. They found no trace of the stray animal, but the cave was far from empty. Tucked in a niche lay a hoard of jars, and in the jars were some scrolls and fragments of parchment. The tribesmen had stumbled upon the greatest manuscript find of modern times.

Written just before and during the time of Jesus, these documents were the oldest Jewish writings ever discovered. They would come to be known as the Dead Sea Scrolls.

For theologians studying the roots of Christianity, the scrolls would have a huge impact. For scholars of Jesus' miracles in particular, they offered a chance to do what they must have thought impossible, to see inside the minds of first-century Jews, and to understand the miracles from their perspective, their unique mindset.

The caves at Qumran where the Dead Sea Scrolls were discovered.

The authors of the Dead Sea Scrolls were members of a community of religious men called the Essenes, who lived a strict – in modern terms 'monastic' – life on the plateau just above the caves, between Jericho and En-gedi. They were led by a prominent priest known in the texts as the 'Teacher of Righteousness'. The Greek word *Essenoi* is thought to come from the Aramaic for 'pious', and they were certainly that.

Was Jesus an Essene?

The idea that Jesus was himself a member of the Essenes goes back three hundred years to the German Enlightenment, when a scholar called Johann Georg Wachter attributed Jesus' miracle-working power to training by the Essenes. At around the same time, the notion that John the Baptist was an Essene also surfaced.

Over the centuries, this fringe area of biblical study has produced some intriguing arguments: the angels at the annunciation and resurrection were actually white-robed Essenes orchestrating the whole thing; the last supper was not a Passover meal, but in fact an Essene ritual meal eaten in an Essene guest house.

At first glance, the links between Jesus, John the Baptist and this ultra-observant religious group seem tantalizing. There is the emphasis on living a life of poverty, and their urgent sense of living in the 'end times'. They also have technical, theological terms in common, such as 'sons of light' and the concept of the 'Holy Spirit'.

Many scholars believe Jesus makes a favourable reference to the Essenes in Matthew's Gospel, when he says that 'Some are eunuchs because they were born that way; others were made that way by men; and others have renounced marriage because of the kingdom of heaven. The one who can accept this should accept it.'

However, most scholars now believe that the differences between John, Jesus and the Essenes far outweigh the similarities. John the Baptist, though he lived an ascetic life, was not as extreme as the Essenes. They cut themselves off from the rest of society, whereas John worked among sinners and outcasts. John's baptism rite was a once-in-a-lifetime event, whereas the Essenes – like many observant Jews of the time – used their water ceremony regularly.

Jesus, like John, mixed with outcasts, sinners and non-Jews, and allowed no hierarchy among his disciples, whereas the Essene life was kept for the initiates only.

One very telling distinction is that the Essenes were a group of men. Although some wives were allowed – when a new member was already married – there was no role for women. Jesus and John, however, both worked with and befriended women.

So, although there may be points of contact between Christianity and Essene teaching, there's no evidence that Jesus was ever a member of the group.

A fragment of the War Scroll, which reveals the confidence of the Jewish people despite Roman oppression.

An Essene 'monk' would hold no private property and live a simple life of poverty working mainly on the land, harvesting dates or keeping bees. He would wear white linen, use no oils on his skin, and in all likelihood he would be single.

There is evidence that some new members brought wives into the community, but most Essenes were strictly celibate. The majority of the members lived in caves, tents or simple huts, and the buildings were used for communal meals, shared worship, ritual bathing for purity, and study.

Those buildings now lie in ruins, but two thousand years ago it was a major complex – a place of prayer and ritual observance, but also a place where work was done. One building identified by archaeologists was a scriptorium, in which the Essenes painstakingly copied out the Jewish scriptures.

In the years following the 1947 find, more scrolls were unearthed in caves along the Dead Sea shore. There were copies of the book of Isaiah, a manual of discipline, a commentary on Habakkuk and fragments of numerous other documents. There was even a scroll called 'Thanksgiving Hymns', which is a copy of the Essenes' own community prayer book. One cave contained no complete scrolls, but a giant heap of fragments – up to forty thousand pieces – which scholars have been trying to match up ever since.

One of the most exciting finds from the Qumran caves was a document that came to be known as the War Scroll. It is a disturbing text, which shows that first-century Jews believed they were in the midst of a Holy War – an almighty war in fact – between the forces of good and evil. But much of it is written in coded language, a further indication that the stakes at the time were very high. The authorities were ruthless in their suppression of dissent.

The forces of evil referred to in the text were none other than the brutal Romans – coded in the War Scroll under the name *Kittim* – who were occupying Judea at the time, and polluting the hearts and minds of Jews with their decadence and pagan ways. But the note struck by the War Scroll is far from a howl of despair. In fact, it may be closer to a victory cry, because the Jewish people believed that deliverance was just around the corner.

The more scholars pored over the War Scroll, the more surprising its contents appeared to be. The Roman empire was the most powerful military

What became of the Essenes?

Archaeological research and the evidence of the Essenes' own writing in the scrolls suggest that they withdrew to their remote Dead Sea location from Jerusalem, frustrated by what they saw as errant practice by the religious leaders of Judaism.

From that point on, they became a maverick apocalyptic group, focused on the belief that divine deliverance from oppression and occupation was just around the corner. They went through various stages of building and development in their Dead Sea complex, including reconstruction following an earthquake in 31 BC. It seems that some Essenes lived beyond the complex in small communities in major towns and cities, where they lived a strict moral and religious life, but played a role in politics and the world of ideas too. They were attacked by the authorities at various points, but survived all persecutions until finally destroyed by the Romans in AD 68.

The Romans at the time of Jesus

Jesus was born during the reign of the mighty Emperor Augustus, whose domain spread from Asia through Europe and into Africa – across the known world. The population of his vast empire is thought to have reached ninety million, and encompassed cultures as diverse as Britain in the north, modern Libya in the south, and Asia minor in the east. Maintaining social stability was a huge challenge, achieved with a combination of military might, technological superiority and sophisticated political and legal structures.

But there was great religious diversity within the empire too. The Romans at the time of Jesus' birth were pagans, who worshipped a range of gods and goddesses from across the empire. There were Greek gods and Germanic gods and African gods, plus of course the home-grown Roman gods that included the emperor himself. These generally coexisted in the polytheistic culture of the Roman empire, and there were huge regional – and even very local – variations in the range of pagan deities worshipped.

For first-century Jews, there was religious freedom at a surface level – great Jewish festivals were still permitted, and thousands of people continued to descend on the temple in Jerusalem at Passover. There were still rabbis and scriptures and religious law, but the Jewish people had to walk a fine line. Any attempt to turn religious beliefs into social change or political protest, any claim that the Roman empire fell short of justice or righteousness, any whisper of dissent, was met with brutal force.

For Jesus, this background of tension and oppression was to be a shaping influence on his life and death. The empire cast a large shadow over him, from the circumstances of his birth – in a stable in a town called Bethlehem where his parents had travelled for a Roman census – to the manner of his execution, nailed to a cross in Roman style by Roman soldiers. In between, his ministry of teaching and healing is shot through with references to slavery and oppression, to the taxes and currency of the empire, to the demands made by an occupying power. And the way he was received by his fellow Jews was powerfully influenced by their hope and expectation that a messiah would come to overthrow the Romans.

In fact, the Roman empire outlived Jesus' earthly ministry by centuries, becoming a shaping influence – as persecutor and later as champion – in the transformation of the Jesus movement from a tiny Jewish cult into a worldwide faith.

A Roman fresco painting of Venus and Mars.
The Romans at the time of Jesus worshipped
a pantheon of gods and goddesses.

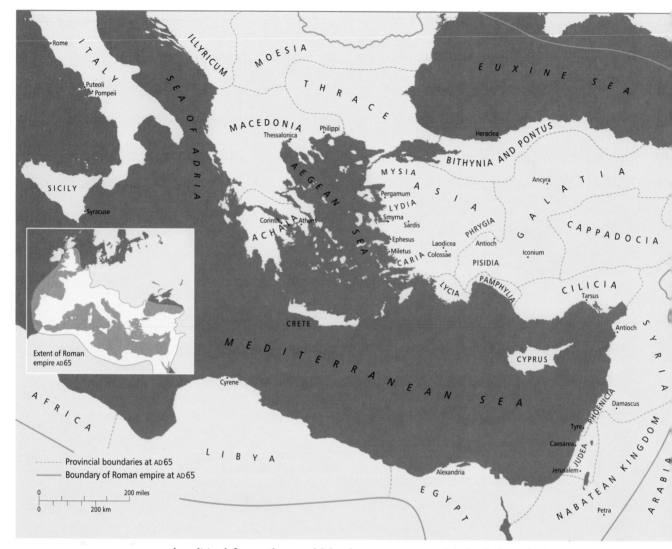

The Roman empire soon after the time of Jesus.

and political force the world had ever seen, and it had the whole region in a stranglehold. But this scroll painted the Jewish people as buoyant and confident, despite straining under the yoke of oppression by a foreign power. And the reason they were confident of liberation against all the odds was that God was on their side.

The scroll looks forward to the arrival of a great prophet, sent by God to preach to the Jews. His mission? To purify the minds of the Jewish people – much as Elijah the famous prophet had done centuries before. Suddenly, the symmetry between Jesus' healing of the widow's son at Nain and Elijah's parallel miracle one thousand years before takes on new power and significance. In a society that longed for the arrival of a 'new Elijah', Jesus' action could not be seen simply as a spontaneous outpouring of compassion. There *was* profound compassion there for the widow in such grief, but there was a deeper layer of significance too.

No wonder the witnesses at Nain were excited. In bringing the widow's son to life again, in performing an act that echoed Elijah so clearly, Jesus was sending a clear signal to the Jewish people that he was the great prophet they had been waiting for.

To the crowds who saw what Jesus did, this was not coded or obscure. They were steeped in the stories of the prophets of the past, and to them the significance of Jesus' act would be as clear as the banner headline on a newspaper. No wonder this miracle provoked a big reaction. The crowds must have thought that the end of the world was at hand.

The discovery of the Dead Sea Scrolls has left us with a unique insight into the complex mix of anger and hope in the minds of Jews in Jesus' time. Without the scrolls, scholars were able to draw the parallel between Jesus and Elijah. With the scrolls, they were able to paint in the rich and colourful background of political and spiritual expectation, and with that background in place, to look at this striking miracle in a different light.

One particular text from the scrolls, known as 4Q52, evokes a strong sense of expectation that a messiah – a deliverer – would come, and that he would be associated with miracles.

'The heavens and the earth will listen to his Messiah, and none therein will stray from the commandments of the holy ones.
Seekers of the Lord, strengthen yourselves in His service!
All you hopeful in (your) heart, will you not find the Lord in this?
For the Lord will consider the pious (Hasidim) and call the righteous by name.
Over the poor His spirit will hover and will renew the faithful with His power.
And He will glorify the pious on the throne of the eternal Kingdom.
He who liberates the captives, restores sight to the blind, straightens the bent.
And forever I will cleave to the hopeful and in His mercy...

*And the fruit will not be delayed
for anyone.
And the Lord will accomplish
glorious things...
For he will heal the wounded, and
revive the dead and bring good
news to the poor.'*

If the miracles were signs, then they
were all the more powerful for it. The
effectiveness of this kind of symbolic
non-verbal communication should
be clear to anyone, even those
who live in sophisticated modern
cultures with instant communication
networks. It is certainly clear to our
politicians and religious leaders, who
know – often from bitter experience –
that their best chosen words are as
nothing compared to the picture of
that handshake, or that kiss, or that
rebuff.

But the symbolic power of the
miracle at Nain made Jesus' action
highly political – a desperately risky
course of action in an occupied
country. Prophets in Jewish history
had a short life-expectancy at the best
of times. Though some Jews clearly
approved of them, many despised
them. After all, a prophet's job was to
denounce sin and lack of faith. Not
surprisingly, many prophets of the
past were stoned to death.

So were all Jesus' miracles meant
to reveal him as a prophet, as the

**In this scene from the
bas-relief frieze
encircling the column
of Trajan, the Emperor
Trajan leads the
Roman soldiers
against the Dacians.**

successor to Elijah? Well, it's not quite as simple as that. There are clear differences being drawn in the gospel account, to make it clear that Jesus is more than just 'the new Elijah'. For one thing, Elijah has to struggle to accomplish the miracle, throwing himself on top of the corpse three times in desperation.

More significantly, Elijah has to plead with God to secure the healing of the boy, as he doesn't have the power to perform the healing himself. Jesus performs the same miracle instantly, without prayer or pleading, and with a simple touch. But if the message of this miracle goes further than a comparison of Jesus with Elijah, where does it point? What more can the miracles tell us, if we unlock their meaning as signs?

Luke's Gospel account records that, after the healing of the widow's son, Jesus is visited by representatives of John the Baptist. The message he sends back to John is that 'The blind receive sight, the lame walk, those who have leprosy are cured, the deaf hear, the dead are raised, and the good news is preached to the poor.' It is quite a list, and it suggests that Jesus' miracles reach far beyond comparisons with Elijah. In fact, some of his other signs would hint at an even more remarkable – and more dangerous – possibility.

CHAPTER THREE:

The new Moses?

The landscape of the Christian story is full of hills and mountains: Mount Tabor is where Jesus is said to have been transfigured – lit up with heavenly radiance – in front of his disciples; the Mount of Olives was the setting for Jesus' entry into Jerusalem, and the reported site of his ascension; and Gethsemane was the place of his betrayal, which set the course for his dramatic final days on earth. Add to this list the location for the Sermon on the Mount, and the high mountain on which we are told Jesus endured one of his temptations by Satan, and a clear pattern can be seen.

But there is another significant hill in the gospel narratives, a lesser-known hill that provided the setting for a remarkable event. The hill has been located on the north-east shore of the Sea of Galilee, and in ancient times it was known as 'the desert'. Today, it is not hard to see how it came by its name. It is a bleak, uninhabited part of the landscape. But the Bible recounts that two thousand years ago, on these dramatic slopes, Jesus fed a hungry crowd.

The feeding of the five thousand has always been one of the most memorable biblical miracles. Although perhaps not as world-changing as the raising of the dead, this apparently practical response to the physical needs of a crowd and the description of how it was done make it a wonderful story.

Jesus does not stand over the meagre loaves and fishes, then magically transform them into a banquet for thousands. Instead, he starts to break the bread and divide the fish and hand them to the crowd. But as he prays, the bread keeps breaking and the fish keeps dividing until everyone is fed. It sounds like a kind of miraculous sleight of hand.

The original account can be found in the Gospel of Mark:

'The apostles gathered round Jesus and reported to him all they had done and taught. Then, because so many people were coming and going that they did not even have a chance to eat, he said to them, "Come with me by yourselves to a quiet place and get some rest." So they went away by themselves in a boat to a solitary place. But many who saw them

Mountains

'Now when he saw the crowds, he went up a mountainside and sat down. His disciples came to him, and he began to teach them, saying: "Blessed are the poor in spirit, for theirs is the kingdom of heaven. Blessed are those who mourn, for they will be comforted. Blessed are the meek, for they will inherit the earth…"'

MATTHEW 5:1–5

That passage from Matthew chapter 5 is the start of the famous Sermon on the Mount, the foundation stone of Christian moral teaching. There is a poetic symmetry here: the ethics of the kingdom – the ethics of Jesus – are handed to the people from a mountain, just as Moses came down from Mount Sinai with the Ten Commandments on tablets of stone.

The religious significance of mountains does not end there. They are of course high ground, a natural 'pulpit' from which to address a crowd, but they are far more than that. In

ancient pagan history, the mountains – or one particular mountain – were often believed to be the home of God or the gods. As such, they were hostile and unapproachable. In Jewish history, Moses climbed Mount Sinai not just to be given laws, but primarily to meet God, and the encounter was so powerful that he came down with his face scorched by the sight of God.

In the New Testament, Jesus takes Peter, James and John with him up 'a high mountain', and is transfigured before them. His clothes become a dazzling white – a dramatic foretaste of the light of heaven and a powerful revelation of Jesus' identity. But it is to another high mountain that Jesus escapes after his baptism, to be tempted by the devil and to work out the nature of his mission. He enters Jerusalem via the Mount of Olives, he is betrayed on the slopes of Gethsemane and is said (in Luke's Gospel and the book of Acts) to return to the Mount of Olives for his ascension.

Yet despite the powerful symbolic significance of mountains, Jesus makes a point – according to John's Gospel – of stressing that God is not to be found or worshipped on any particular mountain. It comes as part of a remarkable conversation between Jesus and a Samaritan woman he meets at a well, where she has come to draw water.

'"Sir," the woman said, "I can see that you are a prophet. Our fathers worshipped on this mountain, but you Jews claim that the place where we must worship is in Jerusalem." Jesus declared, "Believe me, woman, a time is coming when you will worship the Father neither on this mountain nor in Jerusalem. You Samaritans worship what you do not know; we worship what we do know, for salvation is from the Jews. Yet a time is coming and has now come when the true worshippers will worship the Father in spirit and truth, for they are the kind of worshippers the Father seeks. God is spirit, and his worshippers must worship in spirit and in truth."'

JOHN 4:19–24

Mount Tabor in Galilee, the possible site of the transfiguration of Jesus.

leaving recognized them and ran on foot from all the towns and got there ahead of them.

When Jesus landed and saw a large crowd, he had compassion on them because they were like sheep without a shepherd. So he began teaching them many things. By this time, it was late in the day, so his disciples came to him. "This is a remote place," they said, "and it is already very late. Send the people away so that they can go to the surrounding countryside and villages and buy themselves something to eat." But he answered, "You give them something to eat." They said to him, "That would take eight months of a man's wages! Are we to go and spend that much on bread and give it to them to eat?" "How many loaves do you have?" he asked. "Go and see." When they found out, they said, "Five – and two fish."

Then Jesus directed them to have all the people sit down in groups on the green grass. So they sat down in groups of hundreds and fifties. Taking the five loaves and the two fish and looking up to heaven, he gave thanks and broke the loaves. Then he gave them to his disciples to set before the people. He also divided the two

35

fish among them all. They all ate and were satisfied, and the disciples picked up twelve basketfuls of broken pieces of bread and fish. The number of men who had eaten was five thousand.'
MARK 6:30–44

It was late, and the people were hungry. Men, women and children all clamouring for a meal from five loaves and two fish. There have been many theories over the years that attempt to explain away this miracle. Some have claimed that the crowds were whipped into a frenzy of religious fervour on hearing Jesus speak, and that fervour suppressed their appetites.

Others have speculated that the mood of harmony and selflessness spread by Jesus' teaching might have inspired the crowd to offer up their own private supplies of food and share them with each other.

But as with Jesus' healing of the widow's son at Nain, the key element here is the belief of the crowd that a miracle had taken place. They were convinced that from such meagre rations Jesus had fed everyone, and left them all satisfied. As with the miracle at Nain, what the crowd witnessed would have made a huge impact on them, but that impact would come as much from the explosive message – the symbolism contained within the miracle – as from the supernatural feat with the bread and fish.

Reconstruction of the feeding of the five thousand (and pages 34–35).

The feeding of the multitude would put first-century Jews in mind of a towering figure in Jewish history, someone even greater than the prophet Elijah. When those eyewitnesses saw Jesus handing out food, they could not help but think of the father of the Jewish faith himself – Moses. Everything about the miracle, from the setting right down to the smallest details, would suggest a powerful identification of Jesus with Moses. But why?

The Sea of Galilee

John's Gospel refers to 'the Sea of Tiberias'. Luke uses the name 'Lake of Gennesaret', but Matthew and Mark both refer to this stretch of water by its most familiar name, the Sea of Galilee. In the Old Testament, the author of the book of Numbers uses the title 'Sea of Chinnereth', which derives from a Hebrew word for a musical instrument shaped like a harp, a similar shape to the lake itself. In other parts of the Bible it is simply called 'the lake', or 'the sea'.

By any name, this large freshwater lake plays a significant role in the Christian story. Situated below sea level in the northern region of Galilee, the lake is surrounded by hills, which give it a strange and volatile climate. As is often described in the gospels, the lake is susceptible to sudden, sharp storms.

An abundant source of fish, the Sea of Galilee is still an important fishing lake today, and communities have grown up on its fertile shores for centuries. At the time of Jesus – as today – the west bank of the lake in particular was dotted with settlements. Some of those towns and villages played a part in the life and ministry of Jesus and his disciples, and their names have passed into history through the gospels: Gadara, Bethsaida, Capernaum and Magdala.

Fishing boat on the Sea of Galilee.

To unravel this symmetry, we need to go back to the Dead Sea Scrolls and delve deeper into the hopes, fears and expectations of first-century Jews. We have already seen – through discoveries such as the War Scroll – that Jews at the time of Jesus were anticipating the arrival of a great prophet. But the Dead Sea Scrolls reveal that this was only one of several visions of the Messiah.

As scholars unravelled the meaning of the scrolls, it became clear that first-century Jews were looking out for a great military saviour too. This man of war would come to liberate the Jews from Roman oppression. If the great prophet was one crucial agent of their deliverance, come to reignite the passion and conviction of the Jewish people, then the great warrior was another.

It seems that the Jews had a pretty fleshed-out idea of the kind of saviour they were expecting. It would have to be a man with the military and leadership qualities of their greatest military hero. Moses had freed the Hebrews from slavery in Egypt and had led them on the treacherous journey to freedom, through the Sinai wilderness to the edge of the promised land on the River Jordan. It was a spectacular achievement, a cornerstone of Jewish history which is still remembered every year in the Passover festival.

A modern celebration of Passover in Jerusalem.

Jews at the time of Jesus were praying for a military saviour who could do to their Roman oppressors what Moses had done to the

The inhospitable Sinai desert, scene of the miraculous provision of food for God's people.

Egyptians. But this was a tall order for anyone, never mind a miracle worker from the rural northern outpost of Galilee. How on earth could the crowds imagine that Jesus might be the new Moses?

Well, there are vital clues in the detail of the miracle of the loaves and fishes, clues that betray striking symbolic parallels between Jesus and Moses. Those parallels begin where the story begins, when Jesus and his disciples get on a boat, cross the waters of the Sea of Galilee and reach a place the gospels describe as lonely. In fact, they reach a place on the north-east shore of the lake that is so lonely it is known as 'the desert'.

How had Moses' journey to the promised land begun? Well, first he had crossed the waters of the Red Sea, and then he had stopped in the Sinai desert. An interesting parallel perhaps, but not enough to astonish the onlookers.

However, once they reach the desert, Jesus' disciples ask him how two loaves and five fishes are going to feed such a substantial crowd. As soon as Moses reached the Sinai wilderness his Hebrew people asked him what on earth they were going to eat, to sustain them in that barren landscape.

Just before the miracle, Jesus orders the people to sit together in squares of hundreds and fifties. Moses divided his Hebrew people into

Who was Moses?

Moses is one of the Bible's key figures. His role in Jewish history is so great that it takes four major books of the Old Testament to tell his story: Exodus, Leviticus, Numbers and Deuteronomy. That story famously begins with a basket afloat on the river Nile in Egypt. Moses was born a Hebrew slave at a time when the pharaoh had issued a decree to kill all newborn Hebrew males. The king felt threatened by the growth of this immigrant community. Moses' mother, desperate to save her son from the executioners, had placed him on the river in a rush basket, and the child was discovered by none other than the pharaoh's own daughter.

The foundling was taken in by the royal household, and brought up as a prince. He was taught all the wisdom of the Egyptians, and enjoyed all the benefits and privileges of palace life. But on the verge of adulthood, he witnessed a cruel Egyptian overseer victimizing a Hebrew slave. Watching one of his own people die at the hands of this tyrant was too much for the young Moses to bear. In a fit of anger he killed the overseer.

From that moment on he was a hunted man, and he fled into exile where he worked as a shepherd in the desert. But after many years in the desert, he saw the now famous burning bush. Out of the bush came the voice of God himself, telling Moses to go back into Egypt and rescue his people. Moses was reluctant, but he finally agreed and went back to the land of his birth. He confronted the pharaoh and asked him to let the Hebrew slaves go. When the king refused – repeatedly – God brought down a series of terrible plagues through Moses to punish Egypt.

After plagues of blood, frogs, flies, boils, hail, locusts, lice, darkness and animal diseases, the pharaoh still stood fast. God told Moses to prepare for the final plan. At midnight, God would kill all the eldest sons in Egypt. The Hebrews were to eat a special meal of lamb and paint the lamb's blood on their door frames. God would see the blood and 'pass over' the Hebrews' houses, sparing the sons within.

After this terrible night, the pharaoh let the Hebrews go, but he then changed his mind and pursued them right to the edge of the Red Sea. God parted the sea to allow the Hebrews to escape, while the Egyptian chariots were washed away.

In the desert, free but still exiled from their promised land, the Hebrews were led by Moses. He spoke to God, face to face, receiving the Ten Commandments written on tablets of stone on top of Mount Sinai, and for forty years he inspired and shaped the Hebrew people into a nation. But although he glimpsed the promised land, he never set foot on it, dying before his people's journey was complete.

A view across the Jordan Valley to Palestine, from Mount Nebo.

41

companies one hundred, or fifty, strong. In the Old Testament book of Exodus, Moses is advised by his father-in-law, Jethro, to 'select capable men from all the people who fear God, trustworthy men who hate dishonest gain, and appoint them as officials over thousands, hundreds, fifties and tens'.

It's an impressive symmetry, but it doesn't end there. At the climax of the story – the miracle itself – Jesus hands out the loaves and fishes, and somehow manages to multiply them so the food goes to everyone who needs it. Back in the Sinai desert, Moses presided over an equally miraculous multiplication of food. In the mornings the ground was covered with manna – the bread of heaven – like a fall of snow. In the evenings, the skies above the camp were alive with quail. Loaves and fishes, manna and quail: the menu may be different, but the significance would not be lost on a first-century crowd.

According to the Gospel of John, the people tried to mob Jesus after they had witnessed the miracle. That response is hardly surprising, as the possibility had dawned on them that this man could be the great military saviour they were waiting for, the leader who would overcome the Romans and liberate the long-suffering Jewish people.

Was Jesus the new Moses? Well, another more fundamental question is, would the new Moses be able to accomplish the job alone? After all, Moses had led the Hebrew people to the edge of the promised land, but died before they made the final conquest. He got almost within touching distance, to the top of Mount Nebo in modern Jordan, where his people looked out across the land of milk and honey, but he never set foot there himself.

He had freed them from bondage to the pharaohs in Egypt. He had led and sustained them through the years in the wilderness, and had shaped their moral code, their sense of community, their legal system and their pattern of worship. Moses had fashioned these exiled slaves into a people of God, but he was not the man who delivered them into the promised land. That job fell to his successor – Joshua.

It was Joshua, the great general, who assembled the Hebrews on the east bank of the Jordan, and led them across the river into the land of Canaan. And so began the final conquest of the promised land, beginning with that most historic armed struggle, the battle of Jericho.

By the end of his military campaign, Joshua had completed what Moses began. He had given birth to the Jewish nation. The Jewish people of Jesus' time were not just looking for the new Moses. They were waiting for a military saviour who could do to the Romans both what Moses did to the Egyptians and what Joshua had done to the Canaanites. In other words, they were waiting for the man who would reclaim the promised land for the Jewish people.

Could Jesus be seen as the new Moses *and* the new Joshua? Well, there's nothing in the miracle of the loaves and fishes that suggests he was. But that's the way the miracle signs work. No single event gives you the whole picture. According to the gospel accounts, the feeding of the five thousand is immediately followed by another extraordinary feat. And this time, the symbolism all points to Joshua.

FOLLOWING SPREAD:
The Church of the Beatitudes by the Sea of Galilee.

43

CHAPTER FOUR:

The new Joshua?

For first-century Jews, the miracle of the loaves and fishes pointed towards Moses. In feeding the five thousand, Jesus was doing more than satisfying a need. He was giving a sign to indicate that he was the new Moses. The Dead Sea Scrolls make it clear that this new Moses was expected by the Jewish people. More than expected, the new Moses was eagerly awaited, to deliver his oppressed people into freedom and liberate them from their Roman oppressors.

But that was not enough. The crowd knew that Moses – though without question the archetypal leader of the Jewish people – could not have brought them into the promised land without Joshua, his successor. Joshua was the victor in battle, the conqueror of Canaan. So to overthrow the mighty Roman empire, the Jewish people needed not just the new Moses, but the new Joshua too, and there was not a hint of him in the miracle of the loaves and fishes. Could Jesus be the new Joshua?

Well, scholars combing the gospels for signs of Joshua didn't have to read much further to find some fascinating clues.

Immediately after the feeding of the five thousand, the gospels say that Jesus ordered the disciples to get on a boat and go back home to Bethsaida, while he stayed alone to pray on the mountain. But the disciples' voyage back home was not as smooth as they had hoped.

The Sea of Galilee – susceptible to sudden changes in temperature and swift and violent storms – turned from a calm lake into a turbulent sea. The disciples were caught in the middle of the storm, struggling to keep their boat afloat and reach the safety of the shore. According to Mark's Gospel account, Jesus looked up from his prayers and saw his friends in trouble:

'He saw the disciples straining at the oars, because the wind was against them. About the fourth watch of the night he went out to them, walking on the lake. He was about to pass by them, but when they saw him walking on the lake, they thought he was a ghost. They cried out, because they all saw him and were terrified. Immediately he spoke to them and said, "Take courage! It is I. Don't be afraid." Then he climbed into the boat with them, and the wind died down.

They were completely amazed, for they had not understood about the loaves; their hearts were hardened. When they had crossed over, they landed at Gennesaret and anchored there. As soon as they got out of the boat, people recognized Jesus. They ran throughout that whole region and carried the sick on mats to wherever they heard he was. And wherever he went – into villages, towns or countryside – they placed the sick in the market places. They begged him to let them touch even the edge of his cloak, and all who touched him were healed.'

MARK 6:48–56

Who was Joshua?

Joshua was originally called Hoshea, but according to the book of Numbers he was renamed by Moses and became Moses' assistant.

After being sent into Canaan as one of the spies to weigh up the military prospects of taking the promised land, Joshua sides with the unpopular minority view that the Israelites should put all their faith in God and launch a direct attack on the territory. For this faith, God rewards Joshua by telling Moses to make him a second leader of the people. Like Moses, he should be obeyed by everyone.

The biblical books of Numbers and Deuteronomy then outline the process by which God prepared Joshua to succeed Moses. In the book of Joshua, following the death of Moses on the very brink of the promised land, that destiny is fulfilled and, in God's strength, Joshua conquers Canaan.

He leads his armies, priests and people, together with the precious ark of the covenant, miraculously across the river Jordan and into the promised land. God gives Joshua faith, strength and ingenuity to overcome even the heavily fortified city of Jericho, and once the land is taken, Joshua distributes it, dividing it up between the different tribes of Israel.

The gospels say that the disciples were utterly astounded by what they saw. Their reaction is hardly surprising. The image of Jesus calmly walking across a raging sea is so striking that it has become an iconic image. Jesus' walking on water is perhaps the most famous miracle of all. But to understand its meaning, we need to look at the symbolism, and that begins with a key part of Joshua's story.

Following Moses' death, Joshua is responsible for leading the Hebrew people into their promised land. But that final journey looks not only perilous, with enemies ranged against them, but virtually impossible, because the mighty River Jordan lies between the Hebrews and the promised land.

How would they cross it? Joshua was a man of God, and as they waited on the east side of the river, God told him that the Hebrews would cross the water, and in such a dramatic way that they would know they were in God's hands. The story is told in the biblical book of Joshua.

Joshua said to the Israelites, "Come here and listen to the words of the Lord your God. This is how you will know that the living God is among you and that he will certainly drive out before you the Canaanites, Hittites, Hivites, Perizzites, Girgashites, Amorites and Jebusites. See, the ark of the covenant of the Lord of all the earth will go into the Jordan ahead of you. Now then, choose twelve men from the tribes of Israel, one from each tribe. And as soon as the priests who carry the ark of the Lord – the Lord of all the earth – set foot in the Jordan, its waters flowing downstream will be cut off and stand up in a heap."

So when the people broke camp to cross the Jordan, the priests carrying the ark of the covenant went ahead of them. Now the Jordan is in flood all during harvest. Yet as soon as the priests who carried the ark reached the Jordan and their feet touched the water's edge, the water from upstream stopped flowing. It piled up in a heap a great distance away, at a town called Adam in the vicinity of Zarethan, while the water flowing down to the Dead Sea was completely cut off.

So the people crossed over opposite Jericho. The priests who carried the ark of the covenant of the Lord stood firm on dry ground in the middle of the Jordan, while all Israel passed by until the whole nation had completed the crossing on dry ground.'

JOSHUA 3:9–17

What was the ark of the covenant?

The ark was a chest or box which was carried by, and led, the Hebrew people during their years in the wilderness, and became the heart and focus of their worship. At various points in the Old Testament, the identification of the ark with God becomes so strong that to be in the presence of the ark is to be in the presence of God. When Moses talks to the ark, it is as though he talks directly to God.

This clear identification with the presence and power of God accounts for the devastating effect it has on those who try to desecrate it. As the Hebrews approach the promised land, it plays a central role. Carried by twelve priests, it holds back – by the power of God – the waters of the river Jordan so the Israelites can cross. It is carried round the city of Jericho by Joshua and his army, but protected from military threat at all times. Later, it is fought over and hidden.

But when the great King David unifies the tribes of Israel and creates the capital in Jerusalem, he brings the ark to that new capital and makes it the focus of national worship and identity. When Solomon builds his mighty Temple, the ark is brought into the Holy of Holies, and remains there until the Babylonian destruction of Jerusalem in 586 BC. Its location now remains one of the great mysteries to come down from the ancient world. Some believe it is in hiding somewhere in Israel, or in Ethiopia, or in one of numerous other locations. Others believe it was destroyed by the Babylonians.

A reconstruction of Solomon's Temple, showing the location of the ark in the Holy of Holies at the rear.

What did it contain? Well, the Bible tells us it was the portable home of the tablets of stone on which Moses received the Law from God, but there are other suggested contents, including the manna given by God to his exiled people to sustain them in the desert.

49

The battle of Jericho

'Then the Lord said to Joshua, "See, I have delivered Jericho into your hands, along with its king and its fighting men. March around the city once with all the armed men. Do this for six days. Make seven priests carry trumpets of rams' horns in front of the ark. On the seventh day, march around the city seven times, with the priests blowing the trumpets. When you hear them sound a long blast on the trumpets, make all the people give a loud shout; then the wall of the city will collapse and the people will go up, every man straight in."'

JOSHUA 6:2–5

The account of the fall of Jericho in the biblical book of Joshua is one of the most dramatic in the Bible. By the power of God, the Israelites bring down the walls of a great city with prayer and the sound of trumpets or 'shofars'. It is also a defining event in Middle Eastern history, as – according to the biblical accounts – Joshua went on from Jericho to conquer many other cities, culminating in the Hebrews settling in the promised land.

The city of Jericho has always held great strategic importance. It is an oasis town, a rare source of water, and the spring that led to its foundation is still used by its citizens today.

But the accounts of the victory given in the book of Joshua and its biblical neighbour the book of Judges differ in focus. The Israelites believed that God had promised them a land on which to found their nation. The problem was, that land was already occupied by the Canaanites, and the Canaanites were not going to hand it over willingly.

Excavations at Jericho.

The book of Joshua has Moses' heroic right-hand man, Joshua, winning a series of dramatic victories with God on his side, culminating in the conquest of the great city of Jericho, just north of the Dead Sea. He did not rely on military might but on God's power. According to this account, he used great cunning too, sending an advanced party of spies into the city to find out its secrets and weaknesses in preparation for attack.

The book of Judges, however, tells of a much slower invasion, marked by continued skirmishes with Canaanites and Philistines, and the struggles of the Israelites to organize, occupy and rule their 'promised land'.

Modern archaeology has discovered the remains of ancient great mud walls in Jericho. These walls had been built on top of an earlier stone fortification, and it seems that the whole structure did indeed come tumbling down.

At the end of this miraculous crossing, the book of Joshua says that the priests carrying the ark of the covenant stepped up and on to dry ground, and as soon as they did so the waters of the Jordan flooded back into place and ran as they had before. Joshua, his priests and his armies emerged on the far side of the Jordan dry and ready to do battle for Jericho and their promised land. The rest is history, and very well-known history to the Jews of Jesus' time.

But when you look at it alongside Jesus walking on the water, it doesn't seem to add up. How could Jesus make a symbolic connection with Joshua's crossing when he was in the Sea of Galilee, two hundred miles north of the place where Joshua crossed the Jordan? Well, with the developing technology of aerial and underwater surveys, scholars have gained a new insight into Jesus' actions on that stormy night.

The popular view of the River Jordan is that it starts at the southern tip of the Sea of Galilee, and flows all the way south into the Dead Sea. But actually there is more to the River Jordan – quite literally – than meets the eye; a great deal more. The source of the river lies well above the Sea of Galilee, in the Galilean hills in the far north of the country.

Modern Jericho with the hills of the Judean desert behind.

So there *was* a Jordan River in Galilee for Jesus to cross. But there's a problem. He didn't choose to recreate Joshua's great crossing somewhere close to the source, in the Galilean hills. His walking on the water took place right in the middle of the Sea of Galilee. This was a stumbling block for the theory that Jesus was re-enacting Joshua's miracle – until aerial and satellite images changed the way we see the landscape.

Reconstruction of Jesus walking on water.

Examination of those images revealed that as the Jordan enters the Sea of Galilee it doesn't disperse into the lake; it flows through an underwater delta. The strands of river water showed up on the pictures as darker than the surrounding lake. It was unmistakable. If Jesus crossed the Sea of Galilee at its heart, where the disciples were struggling against the elements, then he was also crossing the River Jordan. But did he really intend to re-enact Joshua's famous crossing?

The episode begins with Jesus and the disciples just after the feeding of the five thousand, on the hill slopes that rise up from the lake. The gospel accounts state that they were on the section of the shore known as the 'desert'. That means they were on the east side of the lake, and therefore on the east side of the River Jordan, just as Joshua had been.

As the disciples watched Jesus walk across the delta, they knew he was a maker of signs and symbols. They had seen how he could turn a healing or a parable into something powerfully resonant, an action with a message about the past and the future. And they had just seen him use a few morsels of food and a hungry crowd to send a clear signal that he was the new Moses. Against such a backdrop it is possible to see how the disciples might come to the conclusion that Jesus was signifying Joshua's famous crossing, especially given that they knew him by a different name. Jesus means 'the Lord saves', but the name 'Jesus' is a Latin translation of the Hebrew original. In Hebrew, his name was Joshua.

Maybe this man they had followed, this simple preacher and healer, was not just the great prophet so eagerly awaited by the Jews. Perhaps he was the longed-for warrior king who would overthrow Roman tyranny and liberate the Jewish people.

As Jesus and his disciples returned to their homes in Capernaum, they may well have been mobbed by crowds as the news spread. After centuries of brutal oppression, there was a glimmer of hope at long last. Was this man Jesus the fulfilment, not only of Elijah, but crucially of Moses and Joshua too?

Emotions must have run high that night in Capernaum. But their excitement would be bittersweet, mixed with doubt and fear. If being a great prophet was a dangerous job, then leading a rebellion against the Roman empire was little short of suicide.

The Romans were tolerant of some aspects of culture and religion in the lands they occupied. People were permitted to worship their own gods, often alongside Roman gods, including the worship of the emperor himself. But Roman tolerance had its limits and political dissent was way beyond them. Jewish rebels were instantly arrested and put to death. Uprisings were stamped out mercilessly before they could take hold.

The historian Josephus records one terrifying example, in which a rebel leader named Theudas managed to inspire thousands of his fellow Jews to gather as an army on the eastern bank of the River Jordan, in a bid to march into Judea and spark a revolution. But before that spark could be lit, Theudas and all his followers were slaughtered by the Romans.

Galilee did have one advantage: it did not fall under the direct control of a Roman governor and was governed on their behalf by the Jewish tetrarch Herod Antipas. But the empire was

The River Jordan at Paneas, not far from its source.

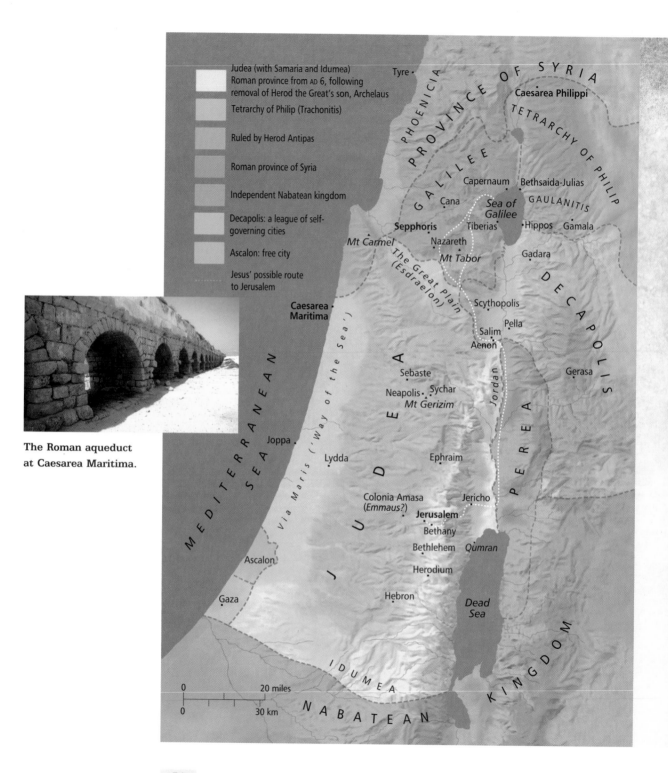

Legend:

Judea (with Samaria and Idumea)
Roman province from AD 6, following
removal of Herod the Great's son, Archelaus

Tetrarchy of Philip (Trachonitis)

Ruled by Herod Antipas

Roman province of Syria

Independent Nabatean kingdom

Decapolis: a league of self-
governing cities

Ascalon: free city

Jesus' possible route
to Jerusalem

PHOENICIA

PROVINCE OF SYRIA

Tyre

Caesarea Philippi

TETRARCHY OF PHILIP

GALILEE

Capernaum   Bethsaida-Julias

Cana   GAULANITIS

Sea of Galilee

Sepphoris   Tiberias   Hippos   Gamala

Mt Carmel   Nazareth

The Great Plain (Esdraelon)   Mt Tabor   Gadara

DECAPOLIS

Scythopolis

Caesarea Maritima   Pella

Salim
Aenon

Sebaste   Gerasa

Neapolis   Sychar

Mt Gerizim   Jordan

MEDITERRANEAN SEA

Via Maris ('Way of the Sea')

Joppa

Lydda   Ephraim   PEREA

Colonia Amasa (Emmaus?)   Jericho

Jerusalem
Bethany

Ascalon   Bethlehem   Qumran

J U D E A

Herodium

Gaza   Hebron   Dead Sea

IDUMEA   NABATEAN KINGDOM

0   20 miles
0   30 km

The Roman aqueduct
at Caesarea Maritima.

Herod

The name Herod still has the power to send a chill down the spine. It will forever be associated with the biblical tyrant who ordered a mass slaughter of newborn boys. By this bloodshed, he hoped to kill a child named Jesus, a child some already called 'King of the Jews'. Although he failed to kill Jesus, he was a man who usually got what he wanted, a man of great political power and cunning who has passed into history as Herod the Great. When he died in 4 BC, the Romans had a problem. Which of the tyrant's three surviving sons should inherit his throne, and become – under Roman watch, of course – the regional governor of this part of the empire?

In the end, Augustus Caesar solved the problem by dividing the territory between the sons, with the one called Antipas becoming governor of Galilee and Perea. It is this Herod – Herod Antipas – who features most in the rest of the New Testament. He served throughout much of Jesus' ministry on earth, and played a hand in his execution.

His private life made him a controversial figure, as he divorced his wife in order to marry Herodias, his own sister-in-law. According to the gospels, it was this marriage that John the Baptist publicly criticized, leading to his imprisonment and eventual execution. Herod Antipas built a new regional capital for himself on the shores of the Sea of Galilee and called it Tiberias after the Roman emperor.

Herod's role in the arrest and trial of Jesus is recounted here by Luke:

'Pilate asked if the man was Galilean. When he learned that Jesus was under Herod's jurisdiction, he sent him to Herod, who was also in Jerusalem at that time. When Herod saw Jesus, he was greatly pleased, because for a long time he had been wanting to see him. From what he had heard about him, he hoped to see him perform some miracle. He plied him with many questions, but Jesus gave him no answer. The chief priests and the teachers of the law were standing there, vehemently accusing him. Then Herod and his soldiers ridiculed and mocked him. Dressing him in an elegant robe, they sent him back to Pilate. That day Herod and Pilate became friends – before this they had been enemies.'

LUKE 23:6–12

Herod was eventually defeated by his powerful and scheming brother-in-law Agrippa, who accused Antipas of crimes against the Roman empire. Herod was arrested and exiled to Gaul, accompanied by his wife Herodias.

The remains of what is believed to be Peter's house in Capernaum.

still in control. The Romans had spies even in this northern outpost. Capernaum – home to Jesus and his disciples – was a small fishing town, but it was also a frontier town.

It is clear from the gospel accounts that the Romans had posted at least one centurion there to keep an eye on things, and this was recently confirmed by archaeologists who found the remains of a Roman barracks and a centurion's house in Capernaum. The news that a charismatic Galilean was stoking up rebellion in the town was precisely the sort of news the Roman authorities wanted to know about.

No one in first-century Galilee would have underestimated the might of the Romans. That might had been oppressing them for longer than anyone could remember. Rome was the most powerful military and political force in history. Jesus' disciples and onlookers must have wondered, as they gazed upon this new Moses, this new Joshua, this military saviour, exactly how he was going to overthrow the Romans.

They didn't have to look far for a glimpse of the answer. It may have come in their home town of Capernaum.

CHAPTER FIVE:

Man and God?

When he healed people, Jesus seemed to do more than just get rid of the symptoms. According to the gospel accounts, he left them with a new sense of wholeness and peace, as in this episode recounted in Mark's Gospel:

'A large crowd followed and pressed around him. And a woman was there who had been subject to bleeding for twelve years. She had suffered a great deal under the care of many doctors and had spent all she had, yet instead of getting better she grew worse. When she heard about Jesus, she came up behind him in the crowd and touched his cloak, because she thought, "If I just touch his clothes, I will be healed." Immediately her bleeding stopped and she felt in her body that she was freed from her suffering. At once Jesus realized that power had gone out from him. He turned around in the crowd and asked, "Who touched my clothes?" "You see the people crowding against you," his disciples answered, "and yet you can ask, 'Who touched me?'" But Jesus kept looking around to see who had done it. Then the woman, knowing what had happened to her, came and fell at his feet and, trembling with fear, told him the whole truth. He said to her, "Daughter, your faith has healed you. Go in peace and be freed from your suffering."'

MARK 5:24–34

As the news of Jesus' remarkable healings spread, more and more people came to hear him and brought their sick and dying loved ones to him. Although Jesus regularly withdrew to be alone and pray, he spent much of the time besieged by desperate people, hanging on his every word. According to the gospels, it was on such a day that one of his most moving healing miracles took place.

Jesus was in the small town of Capernaum, where he and the disciples had made their home. He was teaching inside a house, and the house was packed with people. Mark's Gospel suggests that this was Peter's house. Some of the crowd were locals, but Luke says there were also Pharisees and teachers of the

Capernaum

'They went to Capernaum, and when the Sabbath came, Jesus went into the synagogue and began to teach. The people were amazed at his teaching, because he taught them as one who had authority, not as the teachers of the Law. Just then a man in their synagogue who was possessed by an evil spirit cried out, "What do you want with us, Jesus of Nazareth? Have you come to destroy us? I know who you are – the Holy One of God!" "Be quiet!" said Jesus sternly. "Come out of him!" The evil spirit shook the man violently and came out of him with a shriek. The people were all so amazed that they asked each other, "What is this? A new teaching – and with authority! He even gives orders to evil spirits and they obey him." News about him spread quickly over the whole region of Galilee.'

MARK 1:21–28

This passage from the first chapter of Mark's Gospel is one of many episodes in the gospels

that begins with 'they went to Capernaum', or 'they were in Capernaum', or 'in a house in Capernaum...'.

This small town on the northern shore of the Sea of Galilee is the setting for many of Jesus' healing miracles, as well as much of his teaching, his exorcisms, and some of his early confrontations with authority. Peter and other disciples were said to have lived there and made a living as fishermen on the lake, before meeting Jesus and becoming his followers. Some scholars believe that the healing of the man lowered through the roof to Jesus by his friends – 'Take up your bed and walk!' – took place in Peter's own home.

In the middle of the nineteenth century, archaeologists identified the site of the biblical 'Capernaum' as the modern Tell Hum, and excavations have continued there ever since. One site, on which several small early Christian churches have been built above the ruins of a first-century home, is believed by many to be Peter's house.

Despite – and in part because of – all the miracles that he had performed there, Jesus eventually denounced Capernaum, among other places, for its lack of repentance and faith. Matthew sets out the story in chapter 11 of his Gospel.

'Then Jesus began to denounce the cities in which most of his miracles had been performed, because they did not repent. "Woe to you, Korazin! Woe to you, Bethsaida! If the miracles that were performed in you had been performed in Tyre and Sidon, they would have repented long ago in sackcloth and ashes. But I tell you, it will be more bearable for Tyre and Sidon on the day of judgment than for you. And you, Capernaum, will you be lifted up to the skies? No, you will go down to the depths. If the miracles that were performed in you had been performed in Sodom, it would have remained to this day. But I tell you that it will be more bearable for Sodom on the day of judgment than for you."'

MATTHEW 11:20–24

Remains of the synagogue at Capernaum, the town which was the setting for many of Jesus' healing miracles.

Law there. These officials had travelled from every village in Galilee, and from Judea and Jerusalem, to hear him. They sat and listened, but they had an agenda. This preacher was a maverick, a threat to their authority. There were plenty of rumours about him, but now they had come to see for themselves.

As Luke sets the scene, he adds that 'the power of the Lord was present for him to heal the sick'. Perhaps that power was palpable to some of the onlookers.

'Some men came carrying a paralytic on a mat and tried to take him into the house to lay him before Jesus. When they could not find a way to do this

because of the crowd, they went up on the roof and lowered him on his mat through the tiles into the middle of the crowd, right in front of Jesus.'
LUKE 5:18–19

It is a memorable image – the packed, hushed room disturbed as plaster and dust fall from the ceiling and a paralyzed man is lowered down on a stretcher in front of Jesus. It sounds like an extraordinary feat, to climb onto the roof of a house with a sick man and lower him down. But it is not as hard as it seems.

Many Middle Eastern houses today are built in very much the same way as in Jesus' time. In a town like Capernaum, the houses would be clustered together in an intricate network of courtyards, stairs and rooms interconnected on all levels. Those desperate friends of the paralyzed man could have reached the roof through a neighbouring house. Once there, all they had to do was make a hole. The roof – like many still today – would be made of sticks, straw and mud.

You might think Jesus would be furious, or shocked, when his teaching was interrupted so dramatically. But according to the gospels, his reaction was far from angry, as shown here in Luke's account:

'When Jesus saw their faith, he said "Friend, your sins are forgiven." The Pharisees and the teachers of the law began thinking to themselves, "Who is this fellow who speaks blasphemy? Who can forgive sins but God alone?" Jesus knew what they were thinking and asked, "Why are you thinking

Reconstruction of Jesus healing the paralyzed man.

these things in your hearts? Which is easier: to say, 'Your sins are forgiven,' or to say, 'Get up and walk?' But that you may know that the Son of Man has authority on earth to forgive sins…"

He said to the paralyzed man, "I tell you, get up, take your mat and go home." Immediately he stood up in front of them, took what he had been lying on and went home praising God. Everyone was amazed and gave praise to God. They were filled with awe and said, "We have seen remarkable things today."'

LUKE 5:20–26

Of course, some have argued that the paralyzed man may have suffered from a psychosomatic illness, that his paralysis did not have a physical cause and was therefore more susceptible to suggestion. Many, however, accept that a remarkable healing took place that day in the house at Capernaum.

Typical farmhouses and courtyards in the rural villages of Judea and Samaria. Similar buildings were excavated in sites from biblical times.

Either way, it was another astonishing spectacle from Jesus. It is not hard to imagine the reaction of the onlookers. In Luke's words 'everyone was amazed'. But the reason for their amazement was not the healing itself. To a first-century Jewish audience, the jaw-dropping moment came just before Jesus told the man to take up his mat and walk home.

'Friend, your sins are forgiven.' In the Jewish faith, only one person has the authority to forgive sins, and that is God himself. Of course, people offended by others can choose to forgive them for that offence, but no one can forgive all a man's sins except God. For the Pharisees and teachers of the Law, it confirmed what they suspected about Jesus – that he was a blasphemer.

No mere man could forgive another man's sins. Jesus had crossed a significant and dangerous line in the eyes of the authorities, and he had done it in a crowded public place.

What must his disciples have thought, as they went back to their fishing boats after the people had gone home? First, the message of Jesus' miracles

Who is the 'Son of Man'?

The title 'Son of Man' is used many times in the New Testament. It is almost invariably used by Jesus to refer to himself. Some scholars have interpreted it as a self-effacing term, used by Jesus to indicate that he was the son of a man like everyone else, and therefore referring to himself as simply a human being.

However, there are strong indications in the Bible that the title means something more precise and significant. In the book of Daniel, for example, the term is believed by some scholars to mean Israel itself, but others argue that it has an apocalyptic meaning, painting a picture of the end of the world. Daniel has a vision of the Son of Man that shows him what will happen on the day of judgment:

'As I looked, "thrones were set in place, and the Ancient of Days took his seat... ten thousand times ten thousand stood before him. The court was seated and the books were opened... I looked and there before me was one like a son of man, coming with the clouds of heaven. He approached the Ancient of Days and was led into his presence. He was given authority, glory and sovereign power; all peoples, nations and men of every language worshipped him.'

DANIEL 7:9, 10, 13–14

Jesus uses the title 'Son of Man' a number of times to refer to what he will do in the future. Some of these uses prefigure his own suffering and death, but others – those set at the end of time – show him as a redeemer figure; a saviour, but also a judge.

There is another school of thought which claims that the title 'Son of Man' is a later addition to the sayings of Jesus, added by his followers after the crucifixion and resurrection. In short, there are shelves of books devoted to the meaning and derivation of this title, but no single consensus has emerged among scholars.

What was Leviathan?

Although the word 'Leviathan' is now used to refer to any huge beast or machine, in the Bible it refers to one particular monster. Often depicted in art as multi-headed and dragon-like, Leviathan was a sea monster, referred to in the book of Psalms and in the book of Job.

Evil and rebellious, it dwells in the deep, and feeds on anything, or anyone, it can find. The genesis of this voracious creature lies in ancient pagan mythology, in which it challenges the power of the gods, and is defeated after lengthy battles.

By the time it enters the Bible, the monster has a more complex relationship with God. The God of Israel is so all-powerful that he treats the beast as a plaything, as described in this passage from the book of Job.

'Can you pull in the leviathan with a fishhook or tie down his tongue with a rope? Can you put a cord through his nose or pierce his jaw with a hook? Will he keep begging you for mercy? Will he speak to you with gentle words? Will he make an agreement with you for you to take him as your slave for life? Can you make a pet of him like a bird or put him on a leash for your girls?'

JOB 41:1–5

A representation of Leviathan, the legendary sea monster and symbol of evil.

Leviathan is a vision of pure terror to a fragile man, but a mere toy to Almighty God. Later in the Old Testament – in the book of Isaiah – Leviathan becomes a symbol of the evil and wickedness within the nation of Israel. Once that monster is overcome, Israel itself can be redeemed.

showed him to be a prophet like Elijah, then a great military leader like Moses or Joshua. By forgiving the sins of a paralyzed man was he now acting as if he were God himself? It's a question that must have altered the way the disciples saw another of Jesus' great signs, walking on the water. When they saw Jesus walking on the Sea of Galilee – and thereby crossing the River Jordan – it may have struck them that he was acting out the role of Joshua, who crossed the Jordan to conquer the Canaanites and claim the promised land. If they had understood that by forgiving the sins of the paralyzed man Jesus was claiming to be God, perhaps they would now see another powerfully symbolic strand in Jesus' walking on the water.

Jews who knew the ancient scriptures would have been familiar with the idea that evil dwelt in a fiery hell. But the scriptures made it clear that evil had another home – the sea. One of the most evocative Jewish representations of evil was Leviathan, a monster who dwelt in the sea. And those ancient scriptures did more than locate the sea as a place inhabited by evil. They also set out who has power over that domain. The book of Job said of God, 'He alone stretches out the heavens and treads on the waves of the sea.' He alone? When they saw Jesus acting as Joshua – crossing the River Jordan – close to their boat on the Sea of Galilee, it may have crossed their minds that this was a sign of something even greater. If by walking on the sea Jesus was symbolically trampling evil underfoot, then he was acting as God.

This raises a major question. How conscious was Jesus that his miracles were acting as signs? What was going on in his mind? Did he see himself as a prophet – the new Elijah? As a military saviour like Moses and Joshua? Or did he see himself as God? How clear was his sense of his own role and identity?

To answer that question, we need to understand the language of the healings and exorcisms. They too will need to be decoded by exploring the mindset of first-century Jews.

CHAPTER SIX:

Who did Jesus think he was ?

Christians have always claimed that Jesus was God's only son. And Christians assume that Jesus believed it of himself. But just how safe an assumption is that? Who did Jesus believe he was? By decoding the Bible accounts and reading the clues in his miracles, theologians have tried to answer the question: did Jesus believe that he was the unique Son of God?

Jesus' friends and foes alike were in agreement on one thing – Jesus could work miracles. The theologian Origen quoted an early-second-century pagan called Celsus on the subject of Jesus as a miracle worker, and his miracles also merit a mention in the historian Josephus's *Testimonium Flavanium*. In the second-century apocryphal gospels – such as the 'Infancy Gospel of Thomas' – there are often fanciful descriptions of Jesus' miracle-working activity even as a young child. As we have seen, the Jewish world of Jesus' time was naturally supernatural. For people then, miracles were part of the fabric of life.

So much a part of the fabric, in fact, that it wasn't Jesus' ability to do these things that so astonished them. After all, the first century was full of miracle workers and magicians, and even in provincial Galilee Jesus was not the only charismatic. The historian Josephus cites two characters – Haninah Ben Dosa and Honi the Circle Drawer – as examples of other miracle workers on Jesus' patch. But what really overwhelmed those who witnessed Jesus' miracles was the fact that they were signs, and those signs carried profound meanings.

So far the signs have revealed that Jesus was seen by his contemporaries as a long-awaited saviour. But the precise identity of this saviour has been less clear. Some miracles showed him to be a great prophet like Elijah, heralding a new age of peace and prosperity. Others showed him as a type of political leader like Moses, or a longed-for warrior like Joshua. Perhaps Jesus was the long-awaited Messiah who would set the Jews free from Roman occupation.

However, another famous miracle gives us a glimpse of a third possibility – that Jesus saw himself as more than a prophet, leader or warrior.

As Jesus and the disciples set out on one of their many trips across the Sea of Galilee, they were hit by an unexpected and violent crisis, as recounted here in the Gospel of Mark.

'That day, when evening came, he said to his disciples, "Let us go over to the other side." Leaving the crowd behind, they took him along, just as he was, in the boat. There were also other boats with him. A furious squall came up, and the waves broke over the boat, so that it was nearly swamped.'

MARK 4:35–37

Reconstruction of the storm on the Sea of Galilee.

Certainly this part of the story appears to be accurate. Sudden violent storms from the east in the early evenings of winter are well known in the area. The fisherman here call them Sharkia, Arabic for shark. The disciples are fighting for their lives. So does Jesus join the battle to save the boat? Not according to the Bible account:

Reconstruction of
Jesus calming the
wind and the sea.

'Jesus was in the stern, sleeping on a cushion. The disciples woke him and said to him, "Teacher, don't you care if we drown?" He got up, rebuked the wind and said to the waves, "Quiet! Be still!" Then the wind died down and it was completely calm. He said to his disciples, "Why are you so afraid? Do you still have no faith?" They were terrified and asked each other, "Who is this? Even the wind and the waves obey him!"'
MARK 4:38–41

It's the act of someone with incredible power, and it makes the disciples question who on earth Jesus was. Not surprisingly, the Bible says they are awestruck. Jesus – it appears – can control the very elements...

"Who is this that even the wind and sea obey him?"

Now, of course, from a modern western scientific perspective, the fascinating question is 'what really happened?' Perhaps the storm was about to subside anyway, and the 'miracle' may have been little more than good timing.

But in order to understand the miracle as a sign, we need to focus on the meaning of the event rather than the event itself. That meaning was what left the disciples awestruck. It was more than shocking, it was scandalous.

Once again, the key to unlocking the significance of Jesus' actions lies in the ancient prophecies of the Jews, prophecies that the disciples would have heard in childhood, and were later made to learn by heart. According to these ancient texts there was only one person who had the power to control the stormy seas – God himself.

One passage from the book of Psalms recalls occasions in the history of the Jewish nation when God had used his power to rescue his people, and the

The Psalms

The Psalms are one of the best-loved parts of the Bible, sacred to both Christians and Jews. The book of Psalms is one of the longest in the Bible, containing one hundred and fifty songs or poems evoking or expressing a vast range of emotions before God, from despair and longing to anger and vengeance, to love, acceptance, high praise and repentance.

Traditionally, the Psalms were attributed to David, the great king of ancient Israel — legendary giant slayer, warrior, poet, musician, leader and politician. Indeed, some of the Psalms do sound like personal private prayers, and some do suggest events in the life of David.

Biblical scholars now believe that most of the Psalms were written for worship, and for use in the community. As such they were less like a book of poems and more like a hymnbook, containing hymns for many occasions and using generic terms like 'enemies' to make them adaptable to different groups of worshippers at different times.

For Christians, the Psalms have always been the best-loved book of the Old Testament, and this seems to go right back to the early church. Jesus and his disciples clearly knew the Psalms by heart, and quoted from them.

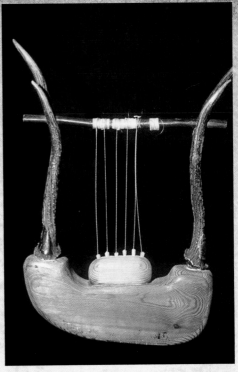

Psalms are poems that are meant to be sung. The lyre was a popular accompaniment in Old Testament times.

way he used that power is strikingly reminiscent of the way Jesus used his power that day on the Sea of Galilee.

The Psalm describes how God's people were in boats in a storm and cried to God for help, and how in response he is said to have stilled the storm and calmed the waves.

'Others went out into the sea in ships;
they were merchants on the mighty waters.
They saw the works of the Lord,
his wonderful deeds in the deep.

The cleansing of the Temple

Jesus casting out the money changers from the Temple is seen by many theologians as the trigger that led to his arrest, trial and execution by the authorities.

The money changers operated in the Temple precincts to collect religious taxes from pilgrims, and to facilitate the trade in birds and animals for sacrifice. In the gospel accounts, Jesus comes across them soon after he arrives in Jerusalem and makes his way to the Temple, the religious heart of the Jewish people.

'Jesus entered the temple area and drove out all who were buying and selling there. He overturned the tables of the money changers and benches of those selling doves. "It is written," he said to them, 'My house will be called a house of prayer,' but you are making it a den of robbers.'"

It would have been an incendiary act in the centre of any town, but for Jesus to do this in the Temple at Jerusalem was powerfully seditious. To do it at Passover – the most important Jewish feast of the year – when the city was swollen with hoards of Jewish pilgrims resenting Roman occupation made it doubly so.

When you factor in the arrival of Jesus at the city in a powerfully symbolic entrance on a donkey, and his growing reputation as a trouble-maker, teacher and healer, it seems inevitable that the force of the law would be brought down against him.

A corner of the Temple platform in Jerusalem.

71

For he spoke and stirred up a tempest that lifted high the waves.
They mounted up to the heavens and went down to the depths;
in their peril their courage melted away.
They reeled and staggered like drunken men;
they were at their wits' end.

Then they cried out to the Lord in their trouble,
and he brought them out of their distress.
He stilled the storm to a whisper;
the waves of the sea were hushed.
They were glad when it grew calm,
and he guided them to their desired haven.

Let them give thanks to the Lord for his unfailing love
and his wonderful deeds for men.
Let them exalt him in the assembly of the people
and praise him in the council of the elders.'

PSALM 107:23–32

The disciples would have made the connection with the Psalms immediately as they watched Jesus command the storm. By rebuking the wind and the sea, Jesus was showing that he had authority over the elements. As only God could claim such authority, Jesus was acting as if he were God.

But for the disciples, that revelation was not to be greeted with unalloyed joy. It was much too complicated for that. They were all too aware that for a Jewish man to act as if he were God could mean two things. Either he really was God in human form, or this was nothing short of blasphemy, and blasphemers were mad or demonic. Either way, they were usually dead before long.

As it has passed down the centuries, the miracle of the stilling of the storm has lost its edge. It has arrived in the twenty-first century as a story to comfort the anxious and afflicted, a familiar metaphor for Christian therapy or meditation groups. But it didn't leave the disciples calm and liberated from their troubles. Far from it.

This raises a difficult issue for believers. There has long been a school of thought that Jesus' betrayal, arrest, trial and death were not only caused, but willed by him.

If orthodox Christian teaching holds that Jesus foresaw and went along with his inevitable (and ultimately redemptive) fate, then there will always be those who claim it was a kind of suicide. The overturning of the money-changers' tables in the Temple in Jerusalem was such an incendiary act in such a sensitive and public place that it has fuelled the 'death-wish' argument over the years.

In the light of the Psalms, the stilling of the storm on the Sea of Galilee seems to raise the same questions. Knowing that the stakes were so high, why would Jesus deliberately act as if he was God, unless he was courting danger and death?

Did this Galilean preacher actually believe he was God? The only way to be sure of an answer is to look inside the mind of Jesus, and the only way to attempt that is to read the trail of signs, clues and symbols left to us in his actions and words recorded in the New Testament.

A passage such as Luke 4:16–30 paints Jesus as being aware of his identity, his role in history, and the significance of miracles.

'He went to Nazareth, where he had been brought up, and on the Sabbath day he went into the synagogue, as was his custom. And he stood up to read. The scroll of the prophet Isaiah was handed to him. Unrolling it, he found the place where it is written:

"The Spirit of the Lord is on me,
because he has anointed me
to preach good news to the poor.
He has sent me to proclaim freedom for the prisoners
and recovery of sight for the blind,
to release the oppressed,
to proclaim the year of the Lord's favour."

Then he rolled up the scroll, gave it back to the attendant and sat down. The eyes of everyone in the synagogue were fastened on him, and he began by saying to them, "Today this scripture is fulfilled in your hearing." All spoke well of him and were amazed at the gracious words that came from his lips. "Isn't this Joseph's son?" they asked. Jesus said to them, "Surely, you will quote this proverb to me: 'Physician, heal yourself! Do here in your home town what we have heard that you did in Capernaum.' "I tell you the truth,"

The Messiah in Jewish teaching

The great founding king of Jewish history was King David. He was the shepherd boy who became a king, the young warrior who slew the giant Goliath. Crucially, he was the man who brought the two separate Jewish kingdoms together, the legendary founder of modern Israel. But according to the Jewish scriptures, he was followed as ruler by a succession of weak, corrupt or plain evil kings, which eventually resulted in the defeat and exile of the Jewish people.

The growth of belief in the Messiah was driven by this line of weak kings. Surely, one day God would send another David – descended from the great king himself – another mighty leader who would overcome their enemies and bring about an age of justice and peace. The word messiah means 'anointed by God', and Old Testament kings were anointed with oil at their coronations, to symbolize that the role – and responsibilities – of king was God-given.

The Jewish scriptures contain vivid evocations of the coming of the Messiah, and of life under his rule. Ezekiel writes that:

'They will be my people, and I will be their God. My servant David will be king over them, and they will all have one shepherd. They will follow my laws and be careful to keep my decrees. They will live in the land I gave to my servant Jacob, the land where your fathers lived. They and their children and their children's children will live there forever, and David my servant will be their prince forever.'

EZEKIEL 37:23–25

And the prophet Isaiah, in one of the most famous and poetic passages in the Old Testament, writes:

'A shoot will come up from the stump of Jesse;
from his roots a Branch will bear fruit.
The Spirit of the Lord will rest on him –
The Spirit of wisdom and of understanding,
The Spirit of counsel and of power,
The Spirit of knowledge and of the fear of the Lord –
And he will delight in the fear of the Lord.

He will not judge by what he sees with his eyes,
Or decide by what he hears with his ears;
But with righteousness he will judge the needy,

With justice he will give decisions for the poor of the earth.
He will strike the earth with the rod of his mouth;
With the breath of his lips he will slay the wicked.
Righteousness will be his belt
And faithfulness the sash round his waist.

The wolf will live with the lamb,
The leopard will lie down with the goat,
The calf and the lion and yearling together;
And a little child will lead them.
The cow will feed with the bear,
Their young will lie down together,
And the lion will eat straw like the ox.
The infant will play near the hole of the cobra,
And the young child put his hand into the viper's nest.
They will neither harm nor destroy
On all my holy mountain,
For the earth will be full of the knowledge of the Lord
As the waters cover the sea.'

ISAIAH 11:1–9

Bethlehem, the birthplace of Jesus and reputedly of King David as well.

When Jesus began to emerge as a charismatic preacher and teacher in the province of Galilee, his followers clearly saw him as the promised Messiah. The gospel writers make it clear that Jesus is descended 'from the line of David', was born in Bethlehem – the reputed birthplace of King David – and was seen as the Messiah by many Jews who believed in him. Jesus himself, however, is seen in the gospel as being rather cautious about the term 'Messiah'. Many Jews expected the Messiah to be a political and military leader who would overthrow the Romans, but Jesus' mission was far wider and far more complex than that. Nonetheless, Christians around the world still know him by the title 'Christ', which is the Greek form of the Hebrew word *messiah*.

75

he continued, "no prophet is accepted in his home town. I assure you that there were many widows in Israel in Elijah's time, when the sky was shut for three and a half years and there was a severe famine throughout the land. Yet Elijah was not sent to any of them, but to a widow in Zarephath in the region of Sidon. And there were many in Israel with leprosy in the time of Elisha the prophet, yet not one of them was cleansed – only Namaan the Syrian." All the people in the synagogue were furious when they heard this. They got up, drove him out of the town, and took him to the brow of the hill on which the town was built, in order to throw him down the cliff. But he walked right through the crowd and went on his way.'

With the evidence of the New Testament, and the new impetus – and greater sense of context – provided by the gradual decoding of the Dead Sea Scrolls, theologians have been able to look harder and deeper into the motivation and meaning behind Jesus' actions. The results have been startling. There are signs that, right from the beginning of his ministry, Jesus' actions were consciously unprecedented, dangerous and forbidden.

CHAPTER SEVEN:

Chosen by God?

Jesus' earthly life and his ministry are two separate concepts. As played out in thousands of nativity plays at Christmas time, his life begins – famously – with a humble birth in a stable to a young virgin mother. This is based on the accounts given in the gospels.

The birth stories in the gospels are then followed by a couple of very cursory descriptions of incidents in Jesus' childhood: one in which the baby Jesus is presented at the Temple in accordance with Jewish ritual and tradition, and another in which the boy Jesus is lost by his parents on a visit to Jerusalem, only to be found engaging in earnest theological debate with the Jewish teachers in the Temple.

Apart from these glimpses, we have no real account of Jesus' childhood or adolescence because the gospel writers were not writing biography in the modern sense. For them, the key task was not to document Jesus' life but to tell the story of his work as a preacher and teacher – his ministry.

The ministry of Jesus begins with the realization that he has a mission that sets him apart from those around him. In the biblical accounts, one extraordinary event shows that as a young man he felt he had been singled out by God.

The gospels say that a man named John was baptizing people in the River Jordan to wash their sins away. Jesus travelled to see him, to be baptized himself.

For the gospel writers this must have been a tricky episode. It suggested not only that Jesus had sinned and needed forgiveness, but also that by baptizing Jesus, John the Baptist was in some way his superior. To record the baptism of Jesus by John risks undermining Jesus' image, and because of this, biblical scholars believe it has the ring of truth. Amid the persecution and struggle of early Christianity, this is not the kind of story the followers of Jesus would want to make up.

This episode is regarded by the gospel writers as the spark that launched Jesus' ministry. But what actually happened at the baptism? And what did it mean?

The gospels say that as Jesus was baptized something remarkable took place. Here's how the evangelist Matthew tells the story:

'Then Jesus came from Galilee to the Jordan to be baptized by John. But John tried to deter him, saying, "I need to be baptized by you, and do you come to me?" Jesus replied, "Let it be so now, it is proper for us to do this to fulfil all righteousness." Then Jesus consented.

As soon as Jesus was baptized, he went up out of the water. At that moment heaven was opened, and he saw the Spirit of God descending like a dove and lighting on him. And a voice from heaven said, "This is my Son, whom I love; with him I am well pleased."'

MATTHEW 3:13–17

The baptism was a turning point for Jesus. From that moment, his ministry really began. But what was it about the experience that transformed him from a Galilean peasant to a man with a strong sense of mission?

In the deserts of Judea anthropologists have documented a profound experience regarded by many people as mystical or religious. In a trance-like state, an individual claims to be filled or overwhelmed by a spiritual force. But in many cases that spiritual force is manifest as a person, and that is what makes it distinctive. Similar kinds of experience have been studied and documented across many of the world's cultures. What they seem to hold in common is a sense of presence, of closeness to God.

Perhaps the moment of baptism was more than just a moving rite of passage for Jesus. Could it be that at the moment of his baptism Jesus experienced a powerful sense of intimacy and relationship with God in which he felt he was singled out for a purpose? Well, the biblical account suggests exactly that. He is said to have seen the heavens torn open, and the spirit of God descend on him like a dove.

'And a voice came from heaven:
"You are my beloved Son, with you I am well pleased."'
MARK 1:11

If the experience of being singled out for a purpose was at the heart of Jesus' baptism, then it might help to explain why in the miracle of the stilling of the storm he seemed to be acting as if he was God.

And it is another key clue in trying to understand how Jesus saw himself.

You don't behave as if you are God unless you feel a very close identification

The death of John the Baptist

A key figure in the Christian story, the forerunner of Jesus, and the only man worthy to baptize him, John met a violent end at the hands of King Herod. This is Mark's account of the events leading up to his death:

'Herod himself had given orders to have John arrested, and he had him bound and put in prison. He did this because of Herodias, his brother Philip's wife, whom he had married. For John had been saying to Herod, "It is not lawful for you to have your brother's wife." So Herodias nursed a grudge against John, and wanted to kill him. But she was not able to, because Herod feared John and protected him, knowing him to be a righteous and holy man. When Herod heard John, he was greatly puzzled; yet he liked to listen to him.

Finally, the opportune time came. On his birthday, Herod gave a banquet for his high officials and military commanders and the leading men of Galilee. When the daughter of Herodias came in and danced, she pleased Herod and his dinner guests. The king said to the girl, "Ask me for anything you want, and I'll give it to you." And he promised her with an oath, "Whatever you ask I will give you, up to half my kingdom."

She went out and said to her mother, "What shall I ask for?" "The head of John the Baptist," she answered. At once, the girl hurried in to the king with the request: "I want you to give me right now the head of John the Baptist on a platter."

Portrayal of John the Baptist, the forerunner of Jesus.

The king was greatly distressed, but because of his oaths and his dinner guests, he did not want to refuse her. So he immediately sent an executioner with orders to bring John's head. The man went, beheaded John in the prison, and brought back his head on a platter. He presented it to the girl, and she gave it to her mother. On hearing of this, John's disciples came and took his body and laid it in a tomb.'

MARK 6:17–29

Baptism

Baptism is a central tenet of Christian ritual and teaching. Some denominations – such as Anglicanism and Roman Catholicism – carry out the baptism of babies and young children, on the basis that these infants should not be excluded from the central rite of admission to the Christian community.

The vows and commitments made by parents and godparents on behalf of the child are usually taken on by the child personally in adolescence when they 'confirm' their baptismal commitment in another rite.

For some Protestant denominations – notably the Baptists – this central Christian act of renewal and rebirth requires full adult commitment to make it authentic. In these traditions, the process of baptism and confirmation are rolled into one, culminating in the total immersion of the believer in a pool or baptistery.

Sometimes, in keeping with the gospel accounts of Jesus' baptism in the river Jordan, this full immersion is performed in a river or the sea. Infant baptism is usually characterized by a less literally symbolic use of water, sprinkling it on a baby's head and marking the baby with the sign of the cross.

The origins of the rite of baptism lie in the practice of some early Jewish sects, but there were similar acts of purification in Mithraism and a number of other pagan traditions.

Always a major theme in Christian art, the baptism of Jesus is usually depicted differently in the eastern and western traditions. The west sees Jesus standing in a shallow river as the baptismal water is poured over his head. Eastern Orthodox icons represent the baptism of Jesus as an act of total immersion.

Reconstruction of Jesus' baptism by John.

with him. Was it at the moment of his baptism that Jesus understood his true identity as the Son of God? Was it a clear fork in the road of his life? Did he step out of the River Jordan with a clear sense of purpose, and consistently conduct himself as if he were God from that moment on? It isn't quite that simple.

Instead, Jesus went off alone into the wilderness for forty days and forty nights, where he is said to have been tempted by the devil.

The harsh wilderness of the Judean desert.

'Then Jesus was led by the Spirit into the desert to be tempted by the devil.

The wilderness in Christian tradition

'The wilderness years', 'out in the wilderness'... The word 'wilderness' is everyday currency now, used to refer to social exile, or to a brief hiatus in the glittering career of a celebrity. It is a powerful image, a word that conjures up images of untamed desert, wild weather and a lack of food and water. Most of all, it carries connotations of isolation, hardship and challenge. In the secular world, this is a grim picture. In Christian tradition, however, the wilderness experience is double-edged.

When Jesus went out into the wilderness following his baptism, it was certainly a place of suffering and temptation. In the gospel accounts, he was tempted by the devil in the wilderness, and that makes a kind of instinctive sense. Where better to tempt a strong-willed man than a place where he is isolated, hungry, hot and thirsty, stripped of all the props and trappings of his life? But Jesus often went into the wilderness to pray, to be alone with God, and – having resisted the devil's temptations – we see him re-enter the world and begin his ministry.

The wilderness occupies a deep and profound place in Jewish history. On their journey from exile in Egypt to their promised land, under Moses' leadership, the Hebrew people spent years in the bleak, empty wastes of Sinai. Here they laid the foundations of a nation, a religion, a people.

For the Essenes who wrote the Dead Sea Scrolls, for John the Baptist and for Jesus himself, the wilderness – or the desert – was a place of challenge, but also a place of a revelation.

In the early centuries of the Christian church, many holy men and women sought out the 'desert' or 'wilderness experience' as a way of imitating Christ, and of coming closer to God. In the third century, St Antony of Egypt gave away all his possessions and went to live in the desert, to pray and fast and wrestle with demons. Such was his influence that many disciples came to live the same life, and St Antony became one of the founding fathers of the monastic movement.

Throughout Christian history, many others have followed Jesus into the wilderness, whether that wilderness is found in the desert of Egypt or the bleak beauty of St Columba's Iona, off the western coast of Scotland, where the wilderness comes in the form of slate grey rocks and a cold sea.

After fasting for forty days and forty nights, he was hungry. The tempter came to him and said, "If you are the Son of God, tell these stones to become bread." Jesus answered, "It is written: 'Man does not live on bread alone, but on every word that comes from the mouth of God.'"

Then the devil took him to the holy city and had him stand on the highest point of the temple. "If you are the Son of God," he said, "throw yourself down. For it is written: 'He will command his angels concerning you, and they will lift you up in their hands, so that you will not strike your foot against a stone.'" Jesus answered him, "It is also written: 'Do not put the Lord your God to the test.'"

Again, the devil took him to a very high mountain and showed him all the kingdoms of the world and their splendour. "All this I will give you," he said, "if you will bow down and worship me." Jesus said to him, "Away from me, Satan! For it is written: 'Worship the Lord your God, and serve him only.'" Then the devil left him, and angels came and attended him.'

MATTHEW 4:1–11

Anthropologists who have studied contemporary examples of life-changing religious experiences have found that the parallels with Jesus' temptation in the desert go well beyond the mystical moment itself.

Their researches have shown that Jesus' wilderness experience is also part of a pattern. This kind of withdrawal from society is a common feature among people who've had an intense religious experience. It seems to be part and parcel of coming to terms with what has happened to them. For some, it seems to be a necessary part of the process, to test if they are possessed by a force for good, or by an evil one.

So by the markers of contemporary anthropology, Jesus' retreat into the wilderness following his baptism bears all the hallmarks of a genuine religious experience.

If he felt that he had been touched in a new way by God, then nothing would be the same again. If his life was going one way it was now radically turned to a new direction. It can't have been easy. But what about his sense of being divine?

We know that many mystics throughout history have felt close to God without feeling they had to pretend to *be* God. Quite the reverse, in fact. The phrase 'playing God' in contemporary culture is reserved for power-crazed tyrants or mad scientists. There is an innate suspicion of anyone who feels they have a unique link with the divine, and a mandate to behave accordingly.

In Jesus' time too, acting as if you were God would arouse great suspicion. Even for a holy man, a Jewish prophet like Elijah and Moses, to claim to be God would be scandalous – nothing short of blasphemy.

Was Jesus unaware of such suspicion? Did he consciously behave as if he was God? If there is an answer, it lies back where we started – in the detail of his miracles.

CHAPTER EIGHT:

God's battle with evil?

On the shores of the Sea of Galilee is a place associated with one of Jesus' most remarkable miracles. Today this town is called Kursi, but in Jesus' time it was known as Gerasa. It was not a Jewish town; in fact devout Jews weren't supposed to go there. Yet it was there that Jesus is said to have encountered a man possessed by horrifying demons.

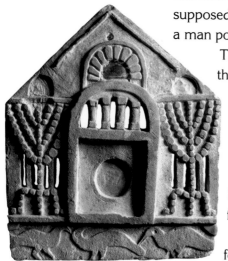

The gospels say that the man – who lived among the caves and tombs there – was tormented by evil spirits. In fact, they say he had so many demons that they called themselves 'Legion'. In the Jewish world of the first century the possessed were social outcasts, forced to live beyond the boundaries of their towns and villages. Coming into contact with such people was believed to make you impure.

Not only that, but to be in a place where there were tombs meant being close to dead bodies, which were avoided by observant Jews for fear of becoming unclean.

In fact, this place was about as far beyond the pale as it could get for a first-century Jew. Jesus was flanked by forces believed to be the enemies of Yahweh and the Jewish people. He was in a very dangerous position. Yet surprisingly Jesus chose to approach the man. And not only that; he chose to help him.

A Jewish limestone tablet from the fifth century. Its purpose was to give protection against demons.

'They went across the lake to the region of the Gerasenes. When Jesus got out of the boat, a man with an evil spirit came from the tombs to meet him. This man lived in the tombs, and no one could bind him any more, not even with a chain. For he had often been chained hand and foot, but he tore the chains apart and broke the irons on his feet. No-one was strong enough to subdue him. Night and day among the tombs and in the hills he would cry out and cut himself with stones.

When he saw Jesus from a distance, he ran and fell on his knees in front of him. He shouted at the top of his voice, "What do you want with me, Jesus, Son of the Most High God? Swear to God that you won't torture me!" For Jesus

Belief in demons

In first-century Judaism, and early Christianity, it was widely believed that evil spirits could take possession of a person and cause mental and physical illnesses, especially symptoms we now associate with epilepsy. By exorcism, which often took the form of words or incantation, the demon might be expelled and the sufferer cured.

The word 'demon' is used sixty-three times in the New Testament, mostly in Mark, Matthew and Luke's Gospels. They are also frequently described in the New Testament as 'unclean spirits', or 'evil spirits'. In first-century Judaism, most demons were believed to live in deserts and were held responsible for illness and natural disasters. These effects are often described in the Old Testament, such as plagues in the book of Hosea, terror in the night in the book of Psalms, and extreme cold in the book of Isaiah.

The effect that demons had on the health of human beings was believed to be extensive, and is described in the Gospels. Matthew chapter 8, Luke chapter 8 and Mark chapter 5 describe demons driving a person to violent, insane behaviour. Matthew, Mark and Luke also ascribe particular incidences of deafness, muteness and blindness to demonic possession. Wherever possession is described, its effects are clear, violent and often long-standing. Matthew describes cases of possessed people being driven to the point of self-harm and even self-destruction.

Although they were not believed to have 'voices', demons were thought to be able to speak through the person they possessed, as in the case at Gerasa. Using a human voice enabled the demons to plead for their own well-being when faced with an exorcist. Apart from their ability to 'speak', demons were believed to take control of a person's whole body, increasing their normal strength and physically resisting any attempt to cast them out.

had said to him, "Come out of this man, you evil spirit!" Then Jesus asked him, "What is your name?" "My name is Legion," he replied, "for we are many." And he begged Jesus again and again not to send them out of the area.

A large herd of pigs was feeding on the nearby hillside. The demons begged Jesus, "Send us among the pigs; allow us to go into them." He gave them permission, and evil spirits came out and went into the pigs. The herd, about two thousand in number, rushed down the steep bank into the lake and were drowned. Those tending the pigs ran off and reported this in the town and countryside, and the people went out to see what had happened.

When they came to Jesus, they saw the man who had been possessed by the legion of demons, sitting there, dressed and in his right mind; and

**Reconstruction of
Jesus casting out
'Legion'.**

*they were afraid. Those who had seen it told the people what had happened
to the demon-possessed man – and told about the pigs as well. Then the
people began to plead with Jesus to leave their region.'*
MARK 5:1–17

Exorcisms still happen today, but they are controversial. Some claim these people are not victims of demons, but rather of what we would term depression or mental illness. For them, an 'exorcism' is not a supernatural phenomenon at all, just the moment when a burden is lifted. Perhaps Jesus' skill had more to do

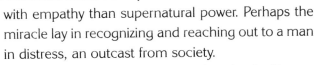

with empathy than supernatural power. Perhaps the miracle lay in recognizing and reaching out to a man in distress, an outcast from society.

But whatever happened on that day in Gerasa, the miracle had far greater significance for those who witnessed it than the release of a poor soul from bondage. And for Jesus himself, it may have signalled something far deeper about his own identity.

There's a clue in the strange fate of the demons. As they left the man, they didn't just disappear. They are said to have entered the bodies of a herd of pigs grazing nearby. The shocked animals then rushed down the hillside into the sea. And this would have made perfect sense to those watching.

First-century Jews knew the ancient scriptures, so they would know that the sea was the home of Satan. If the pigs were possessed by evil spirits, then of course they would plunge into the sea. The demons were returning to their natural habitat.

At Gerasa, it seems, Jesus took on Satan's minions and won. For the disciples, this victory was full of meaning. They knew that not just anyone could triumph over evil. They, like many Jews at the time, had very clear beliefs on how the battle against evil could be won.

To unlock those beliefs and understand the expectations of first-century Jews, the Dead Sea Scrolls, written by the monastic community known as the Essenes, have proved an invaluable source of information and insight for theologians.

As we have already seen, when the scrolls were

pieced together and translated, they revealed that their authors were expecting the imminent victory of good over evil.

They had lived through centuries of oppression. They had been overthrown by foreign powers, taken into exile, and were now ruled by the brutal Romans, who dealt with any hint of opposition ruthlessly. The Jews believed that the Romans were Satan's representatives on earth, and Roman dominance meant that evil had taken root in their land.

It's no wonder then that the Essene scrolls reveal a strong hope that evil would be overcome. That meant the political and military evil of the Roman empire of course, but it also meant supernatural forces, such as the demons who possessed the man at Gerasa.

According to the scrolls there was only one power strong enough to deliver the final victory over evil, the most potent force for good in the universe – God himself.

So, by taking on the demons at Gerasa and banishing them to the sea, was Jesus suggesting he was God? By this stage of his ministry, did he have a clear sense of his own identity?

At first glance it seems far-fetched that a single event could carry so much significance. After all, Jesus had only performed an exorcism, and exorcists were pretty common in the first century. By casting a few demons into the sea Jesus was hardly signalling a monumental battle against Satan.

Exorcists in first-century Judaism

Jesus was not the only exorcist in operation at the time. The gospels make clear that some of the Pharisees and their disciples were exorcists, but in the New Testament Acts of the Apostles, the writer condemns other Jewish exorcists for not working under the same authority as Jesus. In Mark chapter 9, the gospel writer describes a debate between Jesus and some of his disciples on this very issue. ' "Teacher," said John, "we saw a man driving out demons in your name and we told him to stop, because he was not one of us." "Do not stop him," Jesus said. "No-one who does a miracle in my name can in the next moment say anything bad about me, for whoever is not against us is for us." '

Among the scrolls discovered in the Dead Sea caves are several that refer to exorcism. The so-called 'Prayer of Nabonidus' describes Nabuani, the King of Babylon, who had been afflicted with an evil ulcer for seven years, being healed by a Jewish exorcist.

But what if the exorcism at Gerasa was part of a wider pattern? What if this wasn't the only time Jesus confronted the evil powers that lived under the sea?

The search for such a pattern leads us back to one of the most dramatic miracles in the Bible, when Jesus walked on water. It would be an astonishing feat to witness, defying the laws of nature, but as we have seen with so many of Jesus' miracles, the symbolic power of this action was as terrifying as it was exciting. By walking on the sea, Jesus was trampling all over evil.

Following his victory over the Gerasa demons, sending them back to the ocean depths, a pattern was beginning to emerge, and the pattern suggested that Jesus was consciously acting as if he was God.

All too aware that it was scandalous in Jewish society for a mere mortal to suggest he was God on earth, the disciples must have sifted the evidence. How could they be certain of the meaning behind their master's actions? When the stakes were so high, was Jesus really publicly portraying himself as God?

Well, the Dead Sea Scrolls suggest that there were more markers, more signposts that would tell Jesus' followers that God was acting in the world. It wasn't just about confronting evil in its watery home. The Jews were on the lookout for other key signs that would convince them that Jesus believed he was God.

FOLLOWING SPREAD:
The Sea of Galilee
viewed from Golan.

Jesus' exorcisms

According to the gospels, Jesus uses no esoteric techniques to deliver people from the ravages of demonic possession. He simply has the authority over evil spirits to cast them out.

Other Jewish exorcists used magical practices or particular incantations when attempting an exorcism, but Jesus simply issues a command based on his own authority – 'Come out of the man!'

As described in the gospels, the demons immediately understand and respect Jesus' power over them, a power that was regarded both as a sign of the kingdom of God breaking into the here-and-now and as a foretaste of the final defeat of evil by Jesus. Matthew, Mark and Luke all describe Jesus passing this power on to his disciples, and the ministry of exorcism has continued throughout the history of the Christian church. Although the language of 'demon possession' is not widely used in the modern church, there are still Christians who believe in, and practise, exorcism.

CHAPTER NINE:

Return to Eden?

One of the Bible's best-known places is Cana. The precise location of this first-century Galilean village is still the subject of scholarly debate, but the miracle said to have taken place there has passed into popular folklore, recounted and preached about at numerous weddings. The simplicity and joy of this miracle of Jesus make it one that many have since wished to emulate. It is described in the Gospel of John.

'On the third day a wedding took place at Cana in Galilee. Jesus' mother was there, and Jesus and his disciples had also been invited to the wedding. When the wine was gone, Jesus' mother said to him, "They have no more wine." "Dear woman, why do you involve me?" Jesus replied. "My time has not yet come."

His mother said to the servants, "Do whatever he tells you." Nearby stood six stone water jars, the kind used by the Jews for ceremonial washing, each holding from twenty to thirty gallons. Jesus said to the servants, "Fill the jars with water"; so they filled them to the brim. Then he told them, "Now draw some out and take it to the master of the banquet." They did so, and the master of the banquet tasted the water that had been turned into wine. He did not realize where it had come from, though the servants who had drawn the water knew.

Then he called the bridegroom aside and said, "Everyone brings out the choice wine first and then the cheaper wine after the guests have had too much to drink; but you have saved the best till now."'

As John tells it, the story is full of modern resonances. Just like today, first-century Jewish weddings were a cause for celebration, and the whole village was included in the feasting. It would have been quite a party to cater for. So, maybe it is no surprise that the host's wine runs out. Jesus' response seems spontaneous and sympathetic, and 'turning water into wine' is still a phrase that suggests abundance and generosity.

The Gospel records that as a result of the miracle, 'the disciples believed in him'. Of course, sceptics might say Jesus had performed a party trick, albeit a pretty spectacular one. But if it was just a trick, there were some pretty strange elements to it. Magicians revel in the bafflement of their audience, whereas Jesus doesn't tell anyone what he has done. Only the disciples see what's going on. It is hardly the act of a seasoned performer.

The Cana party

Archaeologists have identified three possible sites – two in Israel and one in Lebanon – for the biblical Cana. Each of them has its academic adherents, and each has its share of the pilgrim and tourist markets. It seems likely from the biblical accounts that Cana would be somewhere close to home for Jesus, his mother and his disciples.

There has long been speculation as to the identity of the couple whose marriage was so fulsomely celebrated at Cana. The fact that Mary the mother of Jesus felt it necessary to ask her son if he could solve the catering problem does hint at a familial responsibility. Was this the wedding of a couple within Jesus' (and Mary's) extended family?

A possible site for Cana, where Jesus turned water into wine.

A close family connection seems more than likely, but any step beyond that, any attempt to identify the married couple by name, is grounded on pure speculation. The gospel writer is not interested in the identity of the bride and groom, and leaves no solid clues.

Some of the more outlandish theories have included identifying the bride as Mary Magdalene, and the groom as John the evangelist himself, or even Jesus.

Reconstruction of the
wedding at Cana.

But perhaps it is no wonder Jesus keeps his miracle quiet. For a twentieth-century audience, it would mean far more than the alchemy of turning one liquid into another. Once again, this miracle has shocking symbolic power. What Jesus did revealed even more explicitly who he believed he was.

John's Gospel makes a special point of mentioning that the water jars were overflowing with a superabundance of new wine. The miracle had produced huge amounts, in fact it has been calculated at something close to 120 gallons.

But, as with the feeding of the five thousand, this superabundance had a symbolic meaning. The disciples would have been familiar with the Jewish prophecies, which described a time in which such abundance would be commonplace. There would be plentiful food for everyone and an end to illness and impurities. It was the time they'd all been waiting for, when the rule of Satan would be replaced by the rule of God. It would be nothing short of a return to Eden. And it was clear from the Jewish scriptures and the Dead Sea

Scrolls that only one person would usher in this new age of plenty. It would be God himself.

By producing such large quantities of wine, Jesus was once again acting symbolically, sending out a signal to his disciples. A new age of peace and prosperity was beginning. And it was down to him to usher it in. He seemed to be initiating the return to Paradise. No wonder the Gospel says the disciples believed.

Turning water into wine; walking on water; exorcizing demons – these were all the actions of a man by now certain of his identity. Much more than that, they were acts that first-century Jews expected only God to perform.

But just as his astonished disciples think the meaning of the miracles is growing clear, Jesus does something that calls it all into question. If he is deliberately acting as God, then from now on it isn't the God the disciples thought they knew.

According to the gospel writers, this next miracle even challenges Jesus' own perception of what he is supposed to be doing.

First-century Jewish weddings

Experts believe that, in the absence of evidence for religious ceremonies at first-century Jewish weddings, these occasions were likely to be purely legal and social.

A contract was written up and signed by the two families, and the signing of that document marked the beginning of the wedding. The bride then left her home and went to the home of the bridegroom, accompanied by a cohort of friends and relatives. At the bridegroom's home, the couple would exchange vows, after which the party would start.

As with most modern wedding receptions, this party would revolve around music, dancing, feasting and – crucially in this story – drinking. These wedding parties were also characterized by the recitation of love poems. At the time of Jesus, these parties would be expected to last a full seven days, which helps to explain why the partygoers might have run out of wine.

The food and drink for the guests would be provided by the extended family and friends of the hosts, from their own supplies, as there was no alternative source of 'catering' in the modern sense.

Eden

'Now the Lord had planted a garden in the east, in Eden; and there he put the man he had formed. And the Lord God made all kinds of trees grow out of the ground – trees that were pleasing to the eye and good for food. In the middle of the garden were the tree of life and the tree of the knowledge of good and evil. A river watering the garden flowed from Eden; from there it was separated into four headwaters. The name of the first is the Pishon; it winds through the entire land of Havilah, where there is gold. (The gold of that land is good; aromatic resin and onyx are also there.) The name of the second river is the Gihon; it winds through the entire land of Cush. The name of the third river is the Tigris; it runs along the east side of Asshur. And the fourth river is the Euphrates. The Lord God took the man and put him into the garden of Eden to work it and take care of it. And the Lord God commanded the man, "You are free to eat from any tree in the garden; but you must not eat from the tree of the knowledge of good and evil, for when you eat of it you will surely die." '

GENESIS 2:8–17

That passage from the biblical book of Genesis describes the most famous garden in the world – Eden. It has since become synonymous with plenty, beauty and paradise. It has inspired great works of art and literature, notably **Paradise Lost**, by John Milton, one of the finest poems in English literature.

Eden is mentioned elsewhere in the Jewish scriptures – in Joel, Ezekiel and Isaiah – as a garden of great fertility and majesty, though Joel also pictures it transformed from paradise into a desolate wilderness as part of a warning of what will happen at the end of time.

For centuries, archaeologists and biblical scholars have sought to locate the 'real' or historical site of the garden of Eden. Traditionally, it has been associated with the Mesopotamian plain, in modern Iraq, but there is no clear academic consensus as to its precise location.

If the garden of Eden has passed into popular culture as a vision of paradise, then it comes with certain complications. In the Genesis account, Eve is tempted by evil – in the form of a serpent – into tasting fruit from the forbidden tree of the knowledge of good and evil. From that moment of disobedience to God, Adam and Eve were in a broken relationship with their maker. They were cast out of the garden, and compelled to forge a life for themselves in the fallen world beyond paradise.

The political and social implications of the biblical Eden are still being fought over today. In particular, debates within the Christian church on ecology and the stewardship of the planet, and debates about the role of women, often circle around interpretations of those early chapters of the book of Genesis.

The River Euphrates.

CHAPTER TEN:

The battle with Satan?

According to the New Testament account, Jesus travels to a house in a country north of Galilee known as Tyre – modern-day Lebanon. Although he tries to keep a low profile, he is approached by a woman whose young daughter is possessed by an unclean spirit.

Now by this time Jesus has gained quite a reputation as a healer, so it is perhaps not surprising that she would seek him out for help. But this woman is unlike any other Jesus has previously encountered. The story is told here in the Gospel of Matthew.

'Leaving that place, Jesus withdrew to the region of Tyre and Sidon. A Canaanite woman from that vicinity came to him, crying out, "Lord, Son of David, have mercy on me! My daughter is suffering terribly from demon-possession." Jesus did not answer a word. So his disciples came to him and urged him, "Send her away, for she keeps crying out after us." He answered, "I was sent only to the lost sheep of Israel." The woman came and knelt before him. "Lord, help me!" she said. He replied, "It is not right to take the children's bread and toss it to their dogs." "Yes, Lord," she said, "but even the dogs eat the crumbs that fall from their masters' table." Then Jesus answered, "Woman, you have great faith! Your request is granted." And her daughter was healed from that very hour.'
MATTHEW 15:21–28

Matthew's Gospel says she is a Canaanite, Mark's version that she is a Syro-Phoenician – both terms that mean very little to us today, but that would have meant a great deal to both Jesus and the disciples.

In short, they both indicate that this woman is not Jewish. The woman is a Gentile. And as such she is considered an outsider. She is not one of God's chosen people. To grant such a woman's request would be scandalous and utterly forbidden.

Jesus the healer

In the gospels, Jesus is depicted healing a wide range of illnesses. Some of these are said to be caused by demon possession, such as Matthew's descriptions of cases of blindness, loss of speech and violent self-destruction, Luke's account of epilepsy and Mark's description of deafness. Other healings take place in a context of more familiar 'organic' illnesses, such as skin diseases, paralysis, haemorrhage, withered limbs and fever.

Sometimes, the detail in the healing stories is a compelling part of their claim to be describing real events. Take the gospel account of the healing of a blind man.

'They came to Bethsaida, and some people brought a blind man and begged Jesus to touch him. He took the blind man by the hand and led him outside the village. When he had spit on the man's eyes and put his hands on him, Jesus asked, "Do you see anything?" He looked up and said, "I see people; they look like trees walking around." Once more Jesus put his hands on the man's eyes. Then his eyes were opened, his sight was restored, and he saw everything clearly.'

MARK 8:22—25

The writer and neurologist Oliver Sacks has written about this account from his own experience, commenting that patients who have their sight restored through surgery often find it takes some time to make sense of what their eyes are taking in. There is a flood of new raw visual material, but the brain – unused to making sense of it – finds it initially fragmentary and confusing. The apparent need for a 'double' healing of the blind man seems to ring true from a clinical perspective. From a theological perspective, it reflects the fact that the disciples could only partially see who Jesus was. They would need further help from Jesus to understand his identity fully.

Jesus' first response to her desperate pleading is enigmatic at best, but to modern ears it sounds downright insulting. It makes many contemporary readers uncomfortable to see Jesus referring to a distraught woman as a 'dog', especially when she is pleading with him to help her.

But his answer was not plucked out of the air. It had a history. The word 'dog' was a common first-century Jewish insult against the 'unclean' Gentiles, and whatever its impact on modern sensibilities it certainly would not alarm the disciples. They would hear nothing odd at all in Jesus' reply. He refuses to heal the woman's daughter because she is a non-Jew, a 'dog'. He believes that the 'bread' of his mission is for Jews alone – the true 'children' of God.

Such a response would make most of us give up trying. But according to the gospels, the Syro-Phoenician woman is persistent. And what Jesus does next would leave his disciples horrified and confused. He heals the woman's daughter.

For the disciples this is infinitely more shocking than insulting the woman. Healing a non-Jew is simply unacceptable. It is clear from the gospel accounts that the conviction and humility of the woman moved Jesus to do something none of his followers would have expected or condoned. And from the way it

The Syro-Phoenician woman

Theologians analyzing the gospel accounts of this story have argued that it carries powerful messages on several levels. According to Mark's Gospel, she is Syro-Phoenician, but in Matthew's text she is a Canaanite. The Canaanites in the Hebrew Bible were the sworn religious enemies of Israel, and were to be wiped out at God's command when Israel took possession of the promised land.

The key message seems to be that the woman is marginalized, an outsider in every sense. She is racially an outsider, as a Canaanite or a Syro-Phoenician. She is religiously an outsider, as a non-Jew or Gentile. She is also sexually an outsider, as a woman in a society that regarded women as unreliable witnesses and second-class citizens. This extreme 'outsider' status makes it all the more striking that the woman recognizes Jesus as the son of David, part of a royal Jewish lineage. She even calls him 'Lord'. Given that many of his fellow Jews in the gospels fail to recognise Jesus as the son of David, it is not surprising that Jesus is struck by the woman's perception and acuity.

Matthew's Gospel account gives full expression to Jesus' conversation with the woman, including the reference to the 'dogs'. It has been argued that the early church – concerned as it was with the inclusion of the Gentiles into early Christianity – would not have included this rather 'anti-Gentile' account unless it was grounded in real events.

is told in the gospels, the implication is that Jesus himself is taken by surprise by what he is moved to do.

To understand fully just how outrageous this miracle was, the Dead Sea Scrolls once again provide a rich source of first-century beliefs and expectations. Ancient prophecies predicted that only in the last days would the Gentiles believe in the Jewish God. And even then they wouldn't come to worship him on their own. It would only happen through the example of the Jews.

But the Syro-Phoenician woman's extraordinary faith seems to make Jesus change his mind. As in so many of Jesus' miracles, especially his healings, faith is a key component. Those who are transformed by his hands or his words are often also those who know – apparently intuitively – that this is no ordinary miracle worker; they are people who have seen the face of God in this Galilean

Reconstruction of Jesus' encounter with the Syro-Phoenician woman.

preacher. In the Syro-Phoenician woman, Jesus has glimpsed a conviction that he rarely finds even among the Jews themselves. By healing her daughter he is making a highly controversial statement, but he is also learning more about himself and his role.

To heal a Gentile is to hint at the possibility that they are as good as the Jews. And to hint at that possibility is to open up an even more startling one – that Gentiles too are welcomed into God's kingdom.

Only God himself can decide who is and is not chosen. Now Jesus is making that choice. Once again, he is acting on authority that could only come from God.

Where does that leave us? If he knows he is God, then why does he seem to be taken by surprise when he is moved to act as God? Well, the creeds and traditions of the Christian church say he was fully God and fully human too. He was genuinely touched by the Syro-Phoenician woman's faith, and he acted on it. Was he more human than divine? Was he just a holy man, wrestling with his mission?

If so, then his miracles are utterly baffling. All Jesus' miracles suggest that he was very consciously giving signs to those around him, leaving clues to reveal who he really was. And in the end those signs all point in one direction.

But if he believed he was God, as the symbolic power of his miracles suggests, then he must have known that there was one final battle still to be won.

Jesus had already hinted that he was the expected one, the one who would take on the forces of evil. But his dealings with demons so far were minor skirmishes. The real battle – against Satan himself – was yet to take place. The question was, what form would that battle take?

CHAPTER ELEVEN:

The Suffering Servant?

As Jesus approaches the climax of his mission, it is only natural for him to leave the rural backwater of Galilee where he grew up and head towards Jerusalem. The city is the centre of Jewish religious and political life, and was policed during Jewish festivals by the pagan Romans – Satan's earthly forces.

If Jesus is going to conclude his fight against the powers of evil, then there is no better battlefield. In the eyes of the Jews, Jerusalem should be the holiest place on earth, but since it has been defiled by Roman pagans, it is now the most evil. If there are any lingering doubts in the disciples' minds about whether Jesus is deliberately acting as God, they are about to be dispelled.

Jesus is described approaching the walls of Jerusalem riding on a donkey:

'As they approached Jerusalem and came to Bethphage and Bethany at the Mount of Olives, Jesus sent two of his disciples, saying to them, "Go to the village ahead of you, and just as you enter it, you will find a colt tied there, which no one has ever ridden. Untie it and bring it here. If anyone asks you, 'Why are you doing this?' tell him, 'The Lord needs it and will send it back here shortly.'"

They went and found a colt outside in the street, tied at a doorway. As they untied it, some people standing there asked, "What are you doing, untying that colt?" They answered as Jesus had told them to, and the people let them go. When they brought the colt to Jesus and threw their cloaks over it, he sat on it. Many people spread their cloaks on the road, while others spread branches they had cut in the fields. Those who went ahead and those who followed shouted, "Hosanna! Blessed is he who comes in the name of the Lord!" "Blessed is the coming kingdom of our Father David!" "Hosanna in the highest!" Jesus entered Jerusalem and went to the temple. He looked around at everything, but since it was already late, he went out to Bethany with the Twelve.'

MARK 11:1–11

Riding on a borrowed donkey might sound to us like a practical way of

Jerusalem

The man who founded Jerusalem as a great world city, the religious and political heartland of the Jewish people, is one of the most colourful characters in the Bible – David the guerrilla fighter in the mountains, David the popular hero, David the boy who had stepped in where grown men feared to tread, who faced up to the Philistine giant Goliath and felled him with a slingshot.

David was born at a time when there was no unified Jewish nation. By the time King Saul killed himself in shame after a humiliating defeat by the Philistines, David is ready to fulfil the role God has carved out for him, to take hold of the Jewish people and their land, and forge them into a great nation.

Initially he becomes king of the southern city of Hebron, but he is not recognized beyond the south at first. His political acumen and military skill quickly see him acknowledged as leader of all the widespread tribes of Israel.

Then comes his masterstroke. With his kingship finally in place, he consolidates it by conquering a new city and moving his capital from Hebron in the south to this new location in the centre of the territory, a rather nondescript Jebusite city. Jerusalem is born.

Already, David has achieved more than seemed possible. He has pulled together all the disparate Israelite tribes under his kingship, and founded a capital that would become the most important city in the world. But he does not stop there. In another piece of pure political genius, David moves the ark of the covenant to his new capital and gives it a permanent home. The ark of the covenant is the holiest of all holy objects to the Israelites. It's a portable altar, said to contain the very stones on which God wrote the laws he gave to Moses. For the Jewish people, it's effectively the mobile home of God, and it travels with them. Now they're settled in the promised land, the ark of the covenant can come to rest.

On the day of the glorious procession, when the ark is carried into the capital, David's kingship becomes unshakable. Now, the twelve tribes look to one city as their political and religious centre. David's city. Jerusalem.

Unifier and creator of a nation, in a period we know as the early Iron Age, David ruled ancient Israel from 1010 to 970 BC. His astonishing achievements still resonate with Jewish people today, and Jerusalem is one of the world's great cities.

getting about, but in the first century it was a powerfully symbolic act – and a deeply subversive one too.

Jesus is acting out what the Jewish scriptures say the Messiah will do when he comes to deliver Israel from the pagan forces – he will enter the city on a donkey. The description is clear in this passage from the book of Zechariah.

'Rejoice greatly, O daughter of Zion! See, your king comes to you, righteous and having salvation, gentle and riding on a donkey, on a colt, the foal of a donkey.'
ZECHARIAH 9:9

In the light of such parallels, it is no wonder Jesus is greeted with such enthusiasm as he enters Jerusalem. But his means of transport is not the only highly symbolic act here. His chosen route gave a clear message too.

Many Jews believed that the Temple, which formed the focus of their religious life, was empty of God. They felt it must be, because if God was in the Temple, their land would be free of Roman rule. But rescue was at hand, because ancient texts claimed that God would return to reclaim city and Temple. And they were very specific about how he would do that.

They said he would enter through the East Gate of the city. From clues in the gospel accounts, such as a reference to the road he takes going 'down the Mount of Olives', it is evident that the East Gate is exactly where Jesus came in. In doing so, he is making a very clear, and very public, statement. He is entering Jerusalem in exactly the way the Messiah is supposed to enter the city. The East Gate still exists today. It is blocked up now, and there's a graveyard in front of it. But when Jesus entered through it in the first century, it must have been an electrifying moment. If the disciples had been in any doubt about whether Jesus believed he was God, this dramatic act must have persuaded them.

But if he was God, would he deliver the final victory? Would he take on the forces of evil? And if so, how? The popular expectation was that evil would be crushed by an armed revolt. The Romans would be defeated and Israel would once again be free – under the rule of God.

Many of the crowd welcoming Jesus into Jerusalem – and even the disciples – must have hoped that he was the one to lead the rebellion. But before he arrived in Jerusalem, Jesus had hinted that violence wasn't part of his plan.

Through his teachings, he'd suggested he was going to fight Satan in a very different way: by turning the other cheek, loving his enemies and going the extra mile. It sounds like a sort of pacifism, hardly the way to do battle with the ultimate forces of evil. If the disciples were confused by now, it was about to get a lot worse.

Instead of taking on the Romans and defeating them, within days of his arrival in Jerusalem it seems Jesus has completely given in to them. He is arrested, brought to trial and condemned to death by crucifixion, the most humiliating and painful method of Roman torture.

It must have been a terrible shock, but surely not a complete surprise, to those who knew him well. He had dropped many clues that death was always a part of his plan. At the Last Supper he'd talked about his body and blood, and asked the disciples to remember him. And then in the garden of Gethsemane on the night of his arrest, the gospels say he prayed that he might be spared what was about to happen to him.

He certainly sounded like a man who knew he was going to die. If his followers had not wanted to believe his bleak account of his own death then, they had no choice now. The Romans were famous for their gruelling and barbaric methods of execution. What Jesus was about to endure would be unbearable and humiliating and would leave him no hope of survival. What kind of battle against evil could this be?

In Jewish scripture, there is a precedent for taking on and overcoming evil through suffering. In fact, it sets out very specifically the idea of victory through death. It came from the book of the prophet Isaiah and it described a man who

Isaiah and his fellow prophets

Following the death of King Solomon, the Jewish people were divided between the kingdom of Israel in the north and the kingdom of Judea in the south. Both kingdoms had their prophets.

Amos and Hosea were the first to leave us their writings. Both prophesied in the northern kingdom, though Amos actually came from the south. These prophets did not just address kings, they addressed the people too. Hosea did this in a particularly graphic way. He was deeply critical – like Amos – of the abuse of the poor, but his main concern was with the marriage between God and his people. The people of Israel were being unfaithful to their God, playing around with other gods at the same time – notably Baal, the pagan god of the Canaanites. He railed against Israel for its infidelity. But like many of the prophets, he did not just use words. He enacted his own prophecy by taking a prostitute as his wife, who was then repeatedly unfaithful to him.

In the words of the book of Hosea: 'The Lord said "Go, take to yourself a wife of harlotry and have children of harlotry, for the land commits flagrant harlotry, forsaking the Lord". So he went and took Gomer, the daughter of Diblaim, and she conceived and bore him a son' (Hosea 1:2–3).

Both Amos and Hosea made themselves unpopular by delivering their prophecy with a bitter sting in the tail. Amos listed other nations that allowed the rich to get richer while the poor grew hungry, and he listed the punishments that God meted out on those nations for their sin. But then he told his Jewish audience that they, the people of God, would receive the same punishment. Hosea warned that God would unleash a horrific attack by the Assyrians on Israel, unless God's

Reconstruction of
Roman soldiers fixing
Christ to the cross.

unfaithful bride came back to him. But he offered a tiny chink of hope, that disaster might be averted if they mended their ways immediately.

Around 700 BC, at the same time as Hosea was stirring things up in the northern kingdom, a new and major prophet was emerging in the south. His name was Isaiah. He was raised in the upper echelons of society and was highly educated. His message was as uncompromising as his fellow prophets Amos and Hosea – trust in God, heal your broken relationship with him, or you will pay the price.

But he saved some of his most powerful language to attack the mistreatment of the poor. Like all the prophets, he called people back to the commandments of God, given to Moses on Mount Sinai, and crucially the commandment to 'Love thy neighbour'.

Isaiah did not live to see if the people of God heeded his prophesies and managed to avert catastrophe. Like all the prophets, he was feared and reviled in equal measure, and he felt that his message was largely ignored.

But the prophecy tradition continued. Schools of prophecy were even founded, to train new prophets to advise kings. But many of these became yes-men, denounced by the real thing as 'false prophets'.

would undergo intolerable pain and hardship for the sake of God and righteousness, a man known as the suffering servant:

'He grew up before him like a tender shoot, and like a root out of dry ground. He had no beauty or majesty to attract us to him, nothing in his appearance that we should desire him. He was despised and rejected by men, a man of sorrows, and familiar with suffering. Like one from whom men hide their faces he was despised, and we esteemed him not. Surely he took up our infirmities and carried our sorrows, yet we considered him stricken by God, smitten by him, and afflicted. But he was pierced for our transgressions, he was crushed for our iniquities; the punishment that brought us peace was upon him, and by his wounds we are healed. We all, like sheep, have gone astray, each of us has turned to his own way; and the Lord has laid on him the iniquity of us all. He was oppressed and afflicted, yet he did not open his mouth; he was led like a lamb to the slaughter, and as a sheep before her shearers is silent, so he did not open his mouth. By oppression and judgment he was taken away. And who can speak of his descendants? For he was cut off from the land of the living; for the transgression of my people he was stricken. He was assigned a grave with the wicked, and with the rich in his death, though he had done no violence, nor was any deceit in his mouth.

Yet it was the Lord's will to crush him and cause him to suffer, and though the Lord makes his life a guilt offering, he will see his offspring and prolong his days, and the will of the Lord will prosper in his hand. After the suffering of his soul, he will see the light of life and be satisfied; by his knowledge my righteous servant will justify many, and he will bear their iniquities. Therefore will I give him a portion among the great, and he will divide the spoils with the strong, because he poured out his life unto death, and was numbered with the transgressors. For he bore the sin of many, and made intercession for the transgressors.'

ISAIAH 53:10–12

Second Isaiah

In exile, the people of Israel plumbed the depths. They despaired at the thought that they might never return to their promised land, that Jerusalem might never be rebuilt. Minor prophets such as Haggai and Malachi began to address the crisis, building a messianic hope that David's kingdom would one day be restored.

And it was at this time that many scholars believe that the prophet known as 'Second Isaiah' emerged. Or rather, second, third and possibly fourth Isaiah. Chapters 40 to 66 – roughly the last third of the book of Isaiah – describe detailed events at the end of the exile, some one hundred and fifty years later than the first thirty-nine chapters. Some argue that God gave Isaiah powers to see into the future in this detailed way, but most scholars believe that the latter part of the book was written by a disciple or disciples of the great man. These passages are some of the most beautiful in the Bible. Their message is chiefly a message of hope and joy.

'Hear the word of the Lord,
you who tremble at his word;
Your brothers who hate you,
And exclude you because of my name, have said,
"Let the Lord be glorified,
That we may see your joy!"
Yet they will be put to shame.
Hear that uproar from the city,
Hear that noise from the temple!
It is the sound of the Lord
Repaying his enemies all they deserve.

Before she goes into labour,
She gives birth;
Before the pains come upon her,
She delivers a son.
Who has ever heard of such a thing?
Who has ever seen such things?
Can a country be born in a day
Or a nation be brought forth in a moment?
Yet no sooner is Zion in labour
Than she gives birth to her children.
"Do I bring to the moment of birth
And not give delivery?" says the Lord.
"Do I close up the womb
when I bring to delivery?" says your God.
Rejoice with Jerusalem and be glad for her,
All you who love her;

Rejoice greatly with her,
All you who mourn over her.
For you will nurse and be satisfied
At her comforting breasts;
You will drink deeply
And delight in her overflowing abundance.'

ISAIAH 66:5–11

111

We know from the gospels that throughout his life Jesus quoted from this book of Isaiah – when he was preaching in synagogues and when he was giving sermons on hillsides. Matthew's Gospel explicitly connects the healings of Jesus to this passage in Isaiah in a passage from chapter 8.

'When evening came, many who were demon-possessed were brought to him, and he drove out the spirits with a word and healed all the sick. This was to fulfil what was spoken through the prophet Isaiah: "He took up our infirmities and carried our diseases."'

MATTHEW 8:16–17

There are also close similarities between areas of Jesus' teaching and this biblical text from Isaiah 53. They both talk about the kingdom of God. They both focus on rejection and suffering being part of God's plan.

As he carried the cross through the streets of Jerusalem, it is highly likely that Jesus identified himself with the figure of the suffering servant. He probably knew the verses by heart and as he underwent the beatings, the humiliation and finally crucifixion, he would have remembered the words.

But even if Jesus did identify with the suffering servant, how did he think he would overcome evil through such an identification? As he hung on the cross, it looked a lot more like defeat than victory. And it is no surprise that Mark's Gospel reports that Jesus' final words were words of despair:

'And at the ninth hour Jesus cried out in a loud voice, "Eloi, Eloi, lama sabachthani", which means, "My God, my God, why have you forsaken me?"'
MARK 15:34

If Jesus truly believed he was God and that he could win the battle against Satan, then death could not possibly be the end of the story. And yet, as those closest to him watched him die, the Romans were still reigning supreme. Nothing had changed.

It looked as though Jesus had gambled, and lost. All those miracles signposting that he was God, that he was the Messiah, the promised one, and here was his whipped and beaten corpse, nailed to a tree.

The Gospel of Mark describes a scene of such desolation as he hung there that the claims of Jesus' followers – that he healed and saved people – were taken and used in mockery against him:

'The chief priests and the teachers of the law mocked him among themselves. "He saved others," they said, "but he can't save himself! Let this Christ, this King of Israel, come down now from the cross, that we may see and believe." Those crucified with him also heaped insults upon him.'
MARK 15:31–32

FOLLOWING SPREAD:
The Temple Mount, Jerusalem.

113

CHAPTER TWELVE:

The greatest miracle of all?

If Jesus' miracles were signs or clues to his identity, then his followers must have had a growing sense of excited anticipation as his teaching, preaching and healing hit its climax. In his final months and weeks, which culminated in his arrival in Jerusalem and a showdown with the Jewish and Roman authorities, they must have felt that those signs were finally being fulfilled.

Here, at last, was the prophetic voice with the timbre of Elijah's voice, speaking hard truths to those in political and religious power. Here, at last, was the leader who would take up the mantle of Moses and Joshua, who would foment revolution, overthrow Roman tyranny and liberate the people of Israel. All those signs were there in his miracles; all those identities, all those hopes.

What then must those followers have thought, as he hung from a bare wooden cross with nails through his hands and his feet, defeated and dying. In those desperate hours, he must have looked more like another deluded rebel who had got it badly wrong; just another young man with big ideas who had underestimated Roman power. Even his closest disciples must have agonized. Who exactly had Jesus been? And what was his life about?

The gospels claim that the answer came three days later, when the executed Jesus was physically resurrected. That twist in the tale, say the evangelists, made Jesus none other than the Son of God.

And on the back of that belief, a great world religion was built. Without the feeding of the five thousand or the walking on water, we'd still have Christianity. But without the resurrection, it would be just a minor cult in first-century Judaism. This one miracle – more than any other – changed the world, and if the miracles are signs, then the resurrection is the most important sign of all. To understand it, we need to examine its effects.

It begins with a young man's body hanging from a cross. His followers are leaderless and aimless. Their new movement which promised so much is now on the verge of extinction. Yet three days later the belief began to spread that this man had risen from the dead. Not only does this idea take hold among his followers, it explodes into a movement that wins converts across the Roman empire.

Its missionaries are persecuted without mercy, but to the amazement of onlookers they seem unafraid of death, so strong is their belief in the resurrection of their leader. These Christians become martyrs in ever increasing numbers. Yet all the time their movement grows and grows, until it finally becomes the official religion of the Roman empire, sanctioned and nurtured by an emperor – Constantine – who becomes a Christian himself. What could account for that extraordinary transformation? What turned a tiny Jewish sect into a worldwide religion?

It all seems to boil down to one event: the resurrection of Jesus. It's the

What was crucifixion like?

Jesus was crucified. What does that mean? It means he died by the most dishonourable, disgraceful method available to the Roman empire, a method reserved for the lowest of criminals. It means that the cross-beam he was forced to carry up the hill was fastened to an upright beam or even a living olive tree, and Jesus was nailed to it with his feet not far above the ground. It means he was stripped naked, and died a slow and agonizing death. It took several days for a crucifixion victim to die, usually from the cumulative impact of cold, exhaustion, hunger, asphyxiation and thirst. In Jesus' case, the victim was already considerably weakened by the scourging he had received before being crucified. The classic pictures of the crucifixion are almost heroic, with the cross standing proud against the sky, but in reality these bodies were left hanging on their crosses for days as a deterrent to others.

Who was Emperor Constantine?

Born in the late third century, Constantine succeeded to
the throne on the death of Emperor Constantius in AD 306,
becoming supreme ruler of the entire empire in AD 312
after beating off a rival. Almost immediately, although not
yet a declared Christian believer himself, Constantine
began to favour and nurture Christianity in his empire.
And Christian morality worked its way into his legislation
and style of leadership. Although still capable of violence
and oppression, he improved the lot of slaves, legislated to
protect the weak and poor, and overhauled some of the
more brutal aspects of the criminal law.

He became heavily involved with the theological rows
and schisms within the early church, setting up councils
of theologians to try to settle them. The Council of Nicea,
which proved to be a defining moment in the formation of
the Christian church, was summoned by the emperor in
AD 325. Although not yet baptized, Constantine himself
presided at Nicea, and the creed which came out of that
Council became the key proclamation of Christian
orthodoxy and is still recited daily in churches across the
world. Constantine shifted his capital from Rome to
Byzantium, which he rebuilt and renamed after himself
(Constantinople) in AD 330.

He struggled throughout his reign to build bridges
between traditional pagans and Christians, but at some
point he made a personal conversion to the Christian
faith. Although he was not baptized until the very end of his life, to
defer baptism was not an unusual convention, and he may have
converted some years before. He had for some years invested
heavily in building churches, and as early as AD 321 he had instated
Sunday as a public holiday. In the Eastern Orthodox church in
particular he is now venerated as a saint.

**A Byzantine mosaic
depicting the Emperor
Constantine.**

118

defining moment in the history of Christianity. Today, in the Church of the Holy Sepulchre in Jerusalem, tourists and pilgrims file past the place where the resurrection is said to have taken place. But what do they make of it? What exactly is the evidence that Jesus was raised from the dead? Did the early Christians, in their despair and disappointment, simply imagine it? Or were they witnesses to a genuine and unprecedented event in human history?

The story of the miracle of Jesus' resurrection is told in all four gospels – Matthew, Mark, Luke and John. According to these accounts, three days on from the death of Jesus some of his female followers – in Mark's account it's Mary Magdalene, Mary the mother of James, and Salome, but it's 'Mary Magdalene and the other Mary' in Matthew – made their way to the tomb to cover the body of Jesus in oils, herbs and spices. This was a traditional way of honouring the dead. But as they stepped inside the tomb they found a heap of clothes where the body should have been. The grave clothes in which Jesus was laid to rest had been shrugged off, and the body was gone. As the women try to make sense of what they have seen, a mysterious figure shrouded in white appears to them. The gospel writer Matthew describes the scene:

'His appearance was like lightning, and his clothes were white as snow. the guards were so afraid of him that they shook and became like dead men. The angel said to the women "Do not be afraid, for I know that you are looking for Jesus, who was crucified. He is not here; he has risen, just as he said. Come and see the place where he lay. Then go quickly and tell his disciples: 'He has risen from the dead and is going ahead of you into Galilee. There you will see him.' Now I have told you." So the women hurried away from the tomb, afraid yet filled with joy, and ran to tell his disciples.'

MATTHEW 28:3–8

Reconstruction showing the angel appearing to the women at the tomb.

The women's experience was followed by a series of appearances by Jesus to those who had known and loved him. Matthew's Gospel tells how, on the way to see the disciples, the women saw Jesus himself coming to meet them.

'Suddenly Jesus met them. "Greetings," he said. They came to him, clasped his feet and worshipped him. Then Jesus said to them, "Do not be afraid. Go and tell my brothers to go to Galilee; there they will see me."'
MATTHEW 28:9–10

Luke's Gospel reports how Jesus also appears to a follower called Cleopas and his companion on the road to Emmaus:

'Now that same day two of them were going to a village called Emmaus, about seven miles from Jerusalem. They were talking with each other about everything that had happened. As they talked and discussed these things with each other, Jesus himself came up and walked along with them: but they were kept from recognizing him. He asked them, "What are you discussing together as you walk along?" They stood still, their faces downcast. One of them, named Cleopas, asked him, "Are you only a visitor to Jerusalem and do not know the things that have happened there in these days?" "What things?" he asked. "About Jesus of Nazareth," they replied. "He was a prophet, powerful in word and deed before God and all the people."'
LUKE 24:13–19

Jesus continues in conversation with the men all the way to Emmaus, and they tell Jesus – as yet unrecognized – the story of his own life and death. Jesus, in return tells them that all they have described was foretold in the scriptures. In Luke's account, it is only when they reach the village that they realize the identity of this talkative stranger.

'As they approached the village to which they were going, Jesus acted as if he were going no further. But they urged him strongly, "Stay with us, for it is nearly evening; the day is almost over." So he went in to stay with them. When he was at the table with them, he took bread, gave thanks, broke it and began to give it to them. Then their eyes were opened and they

The resurrection in art

The resurrection has long been a key theme in Christian painting. In early depictions, artists avoided trying to depict the resurrection body of Jesus. This arose partly out of reverence, but partly out of the narratives themselves. If his closest friends were not able to recognize Jesus at first, then the resurrection body could not be identical with the earthly body.

The challenge this presents to the visual artist is a significant one. Instead of showing the resurrection body, these early Christian artists used symbols to suggest what had taken place: the guards asleep or astonished; the stone rolled away from the tomb's mouth; the Marys discovering the heap of abandoned clothes where the body had been. This approach has been taken up again in recent art, in which the resurrection body itself is alluded to, rather than directly illustrated.

However, the artists of the Middle Ages, the Renaissance and the Baroque period were unafraid to take on the depiction of the resurrection body itself. Some of these paintings surround the risen body with a glowing mandorla, a sort of whole body halo. Many of them show the risen Christ holding a banner proclaiming his resurrection, and sitting on the edge of his empty sarcophagus. The wounds of Christ – nail holes in his hands and feet, and the hole made by the spear thrust into his side – were commonly used as a focus for meditation, and are often depicted in graphic detail.

The resurrection appearances to his disciples have also inspired many paintings, in particular the meeting on the road to Emmaus and the episode known as 'Noli me tangere'. According to John's Gospel, Mary Magdalene was still reeling from the discovery of the empty tomb when she met a man she presumed to be the gardener. Thinking he might know the whereabouts of the body, she asked him what had happened, but as soon as he called her by name, she knew he was the risen Jesus. Overcome with emotion, she reached out to touch him, but he warned her 'noli me tangere', from the Latin meaning 'do not touch me'. This tender moment between Christ and one of his key disciples was the basis for many fine paintings.

Paul

On the outskirts of Jerusalem, about three years after Jesus was crucified, a man called Stephen is dragged in front of a baying crowd on the edge of a cliff. He is questioned, given one last chance to save his life by taking back his 'blasphemy'. He refuses, and is stoned to death by the crowd. Stephen's crime was to be a follower of Jesus, part of a struggling new movement based on the life, death and resurrection of a man regarded by the authorities as a dangerous rebel.

This story is told in the New Testament book of the Acts of the Apostles, but the most telling line is saved for the end, almost as an afterthought. As Stephen dies, the book says 'Saul approved of their killing him.' Saul would indeed approve. He's a hit-man for the religious authorities, an ultra-zealous Jewish keeper of the Law, whose job is to stamp out this fledgling Jesus movement.

Yet a large part of the New Testament is written about or by this man. We now know him as one of the key figures in Christian history. Our information about Paul comes from that biblical book, Acts of the Apostles – believed to be written by the gospel writer Luke – and from Paul's own letters.

Despite horrific setbacks like the execution of Stephen, the Christian church is still spreading, and word reaches Saul that they have got a foothold in Damascus. Gathering a bunch of henchmen, he sets off to sort out this threat once and for all. Little does he know what an eventful journey lies ahead of him. Even today, we use the phrase 'Damascus Road experience' to describe a life-changing event. The book of Acts tells the story like this:

'As he approached Damascus, a light from heaven suddenly flashed about him. And he fell to the ground and heard a voice saying to him, "Saul, Saul, why do you persecute me?" And he said "Who are you Lord?" And he said "I am Jesus, whom you're persecuting; but rise and enter the city, and you will be told what to do." '

Saul is left temporarily blinded and permanently changed. He's welcomed by the Christians, baptized, and begins to prepare for a new life and a new job.

Saul, the scourge of Christians, is now renamed Paul and is taught the rudiments of this new faith. The gospels won't be written for another thirty years, and Paul was not an eyewitness to Jesus' ministry, so it's a steep learning curve. Based at Antioch – the third biggest centre for the fledgling movement – he is soon out on the road, passing on the word to others.

recognized him, and he disappeared from their sight. They asked each other, "Were not our hearts burning within us while he talked with us on the road and opened the Scriptures to us?"'

LUKE 24:28–32

John's Gospel finds Peter and the fishermen working through the night on the Sea of Galilee, but to no avail. They are preparing to come back in with empty nets, when in the half-light of dawn they catch sight of Jesus standing on the shore.

'Early in the morning, Jesus stood on the shore, but the disciples did not realize that it was Jesus. He called out to them, "Friends, haven't you any fish?" "No," they answered. He said, "Throw your net on the right side of the boat and you will find some." When they did, they were unable to haul the net in because of the large number of fish. Then the disciple whom Jesus loved said to Peter, "It is the Lord!"

As soon as Simon Peter heard him say, "It is the Lord," he wrapped his outer garment around him (for he had taken it off) and jumped into the water. The other disciples followed him in the boat, towing the net full of fish, for they were not far from the shore, about a hundred yards. When they landed, they saw a fire of burning coals there with fish on it, and some bread. Jesus said to them, "Bring some of the fish you have just caught." Simon Peter climbed aboard and dragged the net ashore. It was full of large fish, 153, but even with so many the net was not torn.

Jesus said to them, "Come and have breakfast." None of the disciples dared to ask him, "Who are you?" They knew it was the Lord. Jesus came, took bread and gave it to them, and did the same with the fish. This was now the third time Jesus appeared to his disciples after he was raised from the dead.'

JOHN 21:4–14

Biblical theologians believe that the earliest written account of the resurrection, and of the resurrection appearances in particular, is in Paul's first letter to the Corinthians, written around twenty years after the events described, even before Mark's Gospel. Paul includes his own encounter with the risen Christ on the road to Damascus among Jesus' resurrection appearances. That

Paul's missionary journeys

Before Paul began his missionary work, the vast majority of Christian converts had been observant Jews, who were circumcised and kept all the dietary laws. A Jew born and raised in Gentile territory, Paul set his sights much wider. When he converted non-Jews to the faith, he told them they didn't need to live as Jews. They didn't need to be circumcised – the ancient sign of God's covenant with Abraham – and they didn't need to keep the food laws given to Moses. All they had to do was believe in Jesus, and follow him. But this message was controversial to say the least. In the synagogues of Syria, Paul was seen as playing fast and loose with vital tenets of Judaism and his message soon led to wrangling with the Christian church in Jerusalem – including Jesus' own brother James and the disciple Peter.

However, Paul's missionary work soon slipped into a higher gear and he spread the word far and wide to Gentiles. Paul was a firebrand. The same grit and edge that made him the toughest of persecutors made him the fiercest defender of the faith. Everywhere he went, he made his mark, winning converts and making enemies with his uncompromising message. For Paul, compromise was unthinkable. His belief was absolute. Jesus has changed everything, and now we do not need the Law. The Law was good, but now all we need is faith in Jesus Christ, to heal our relationship with God.

With this message, and with seemingly boundless energy, Paul embarked on three great missionary journeys, travelling from Antioch past Thessalonica in Greece to Athens and across to Corinth, through Ephesus in modern Turkey and then back to Jerusalem. The elaborate transport and communications systems of the Roman empire made such journeys possible for the first time in history, and Paul used them to the full.

Paul's relentless travels continued, despite shipwrecks, brushes with the authorities, and even spells in jail for stirring up trouble. He was unafraid to walk into the toughest, most notorious towns in the Roman empire – even Corinth, a cosmopolitan port with a reputation for being one big red-light district. And when he left these brand new churches, these tender young shoots, he nurtured them with letters, trying to answer any problems and questions that had come up since he left. And he wasn't afraid to set them straight when they wandered off the Christian path. Many of these converts were former pagans with pretty colourful lifestyles, and Paul tried to rein them in.

The tone of his letters is so direct at times that it causes offence even today. In particular, his references to sexuality and to the role of women are still the subject of heated arguments within the church and beyond it. For the Corinthian church, Paul has this advice: 'If a woman will not veil herself, then she should cut off her hair; but if it is disgraceful for a woman to be shorn or shaven, let her wear a veil. For a man ought not to cover his head, since he is the image and glory of God; but woman is the glory of man.'

Eventually, Paul reached the ultimate goal of his missionary journeys – Rome, the capital of the whole empire. Here, as ever, he made an impact, and his letter to the Roman church is generally regarded as one of the most powerful and profound books in the New Testament. But Rome may have been Paul's undoing too. Although there's no clear evidence in the Bible, most scholars believe that Paul was imprisoned again in Rome, and died there.

The route of Paul's missionary journey from Antioch to Corinth.

125

A copy of an extract from one of Paul's letters.

encounter changed Paul's life, and changed the course of Christian history.

'For what I received I passed on to you as of first importance: that Christ died for our sins according to the Scriptures, that he was buried, that he was raised on the third day according to the Scriptures, and that he appeared to Peter and then to the Twelve. After that, he appeared to more than five hundred of the brothers at the same time, most of whom are still living, though some have fallen asleep. Then he appeared to James, then to all the apostles, and last of all he appeared to me also, as to one abnormally born.'

1 CORINTHIANS 15:3–8

According to Paul, Jesus is said to have appeared to more than five hundred people in total. And that is the historical evidence on which the resurrection is based – an empty tomb and several dramatic appearances by the risen Jesus to his disciples. The idea that a man could be raised from the dead has been a stumbling block to many believers, and a source of scepticism to many unbelievers. Is it possible that the whole thing was based on a mistake? Did the women go to the wrong tomb? Did the disciples imagine the whole thing?

Well, the truth claims for the resurrection begin with the empty tomb, left vacant by the dead man who walked away. And there are tombs from the time of Jesus still left in Jerusalem. These have helped archaeologists to answer questions about some details, like the size and shape of the stone that was rolled away from the mouth of the tomb. But there are some scholars who regard the study of tombs like this as utterly irrelevant to any investigation into the resurrection. For them, the resurrection story falls down even before it reaches the tomb. According to this theory, the body of Jesus was never in the tomb in the first place.

CHAPTER THIRTEEN

Was the tomb empty?

In 1968, a team of builders was hard at work laying foundations for some new houses and roads in Giv'at Ha'mivtar, a suburb of north Jerusalem. At the time, the whole area was a wasteland, and the builders were digging it up in preparation for this new development. One morning they stumbled across something unusual. They suspected it might be important, so they called in experts to advise them. The experts confirmed that they had found an ancient tomb.

But the most amazing discovery was yet to come. When they looked inside the tomb, archaeologists discovered an ossuary – a stone box – containing bones from the time of Jesus. It was the custom in Jesus' time for the bones of the dead to be removed from their tomb after six to twenty-four months, and placed in an ossuary to make the tomb available for other corpses.

Ossuary bearing the Aramaic inscription, 'James, son of Joseph, brother of Jesus'.

In this particular ossuary, the archaeologists found one bone that particularly caught their attention. What made this bone distinctive was the rusty nail still lodged in it. After further investigation, they established that these were the remains of a crucified man called Jehohannan.

For the archaeologists, it was a breakthrough moment. Jehohannan was the first victim of crucifixion ever found in Israel. Experts at the time believed he would be the first of many, because the records showed that the Romans had crucified thousands of Jewish rebels.

Yet to their surprise, after nearly four more decades of digging, no more victims of crucifixion have ever been found. Why not? In Tel Aviv, curators at the Israel Antiquities Authority museum had a unique opportunity to find out. They have access to an extensive collection of Jewish ossuaries from the time of Jesus. Surely among all these examples there must be a clue as to what became of all the crucifixion victims. But despite combing through every ossuary, the Tel Aviv experts did not find any bones that suggested the victim had been crucified.

The implications of this lack of evidence were unsettling. One of the central tenets of Christian history was under threat, and the case for the resurrection of Jesus potentially undermined. The logic was clear. If the bones of crucified rebels were not ending up in ossuaries, then perhaps it was because the original victims were not being placed in tombs in the first place. And if that were true then was it possible that the body of Jesus was never placed in a tomb? Perhaps his tomb was found to be empty by his followers simply because it was never occupied at all?

If that is the case, then it raises a big question: where, if not in a tomb, did the bodies of Jewish rebels like Jesus finish up? To answer that one, archaeologists began to hunt in the unlikeliest locations. Just south of the city of Jerusalem is one such place. Today it is a park, but from the evidence of chiselling all over the rock face, it is clear to archaeologists that this was once a quarry. At the time of Jesus, quarries had a dual purpose. Not only were they used to cut stone for building, they were also used by the Romans for public executions. Historians now believe that Jesus would have been crucified in just such a quarry. But places like this served other purposes too. The remains of some tombs hewn from the rock suggest that people were not just killed here, they were buried too. Was this the fate of Jesus' body, to be placed in a simple quarry tomb close to the place where he died?

What was the tomb like?

'Very early on the first day of the week, just after sunrise, they were on their way to the tomb and they asked each other, "Who will roll the stone away from the entrance of the tomb?" But when they looked up, they saw that the stone, which was very large, had been rolled away.' Mark's account, like those of his fellow gospel writers, is clear on the detail that the stone had been 'rolled away' from the tomb, but what did it mean?

Archaeologists working in the Middle East have found tombs from the time of Jesus with doors that look like huge wheels of stone. This stone was set into a furrow, and could be rolled away from the tomb opening by pushing it up a furrowed slope. The combination of the weight and the slope made this a task for more than one man. Once 'opened', the door could be held open by wedging the stone to hold it in position on the slope. When the wedge was removed, the stone would roll down into place, closing the tomb to the outside world. Many of these tombs were carved into the soft white rock of cliffs and caves.

If the actual tomb of Jesus were ever to be discovered, there would be no identifying mark or title to it, no neat nameplate to solve the mystery. According to the gospel accounts, Jesus' body was placed hurriedly in a new tomb cut for Joseph of Arimathea, but never used by Joseph or any of his family.

Tomb of Queen Helena, similar to the one Jesus' body may have been placed in.

Well, perhaps not, because quarries like this fulfilled yet another purpose for the people of Jesus' time, and even today the local people use it in the same way. Scavenging stray dogs and birds of prey are drawn here not because it is a park, but because one corner is a rubbish dump.

Since the first century, quarries have doubled as city rubbish dumps, but two thousand years ago they were places of execution too. The people who nailed Jesus to the cross were Roman soldiers, and crucifixion was the lowest form of punishment they knew. To suffer the ignominy of dying on a cross marked you out as beneath contempt, an outcast. It is hard to see those soldiers bothering to treat the bodies of their crucified victims with honour and respect. Surely the easiest solution would be to take the bodies down and throw them on the garbage dump, to be dealt with by the dogs and birds.

Maybe that would explain why not a single bone of a crucified rebel was found in all those ossuaries? According to this theory – shocking though it may sound – the body of Jesus never made it to a tomb: it was thrown on a rubbish tip and eaten by dogs. This theory held some sway in the 1990s, but then came the evidence against it – evidence which suggests not only that Jesus' body may not have been thrown

The remains of an ankle bone with a nail in it offer proof that crucifixion did take place in Israel during Roman occupation.

to the dogs, but that his body must have made it to the tomb, exactly as depicted in the gospel accounts. The case begins with the nails themselves.

Jerusalem is a huge city, and there are thousands of tombs still waiting to be excavated. Perhaps that is one reason why only one victim of crucifixion has been found to date. The tombs most likely to have survived were the well-built, well-situated tombs of the wealthy, and they were most unlikely to have been crucified. In fact, there could be numerous tombs of crucifixion victims that remain undiscovered; but even if every last one was found, the odds on finding another bone with a nail through it are remote to say the least.

The truth is that most rebels were not nailed to their crosses, but tied to them. Some would have been nailed to their crosses – it was a Roman practice

– but historians believe there is little chance of finding any of their remains. The reason is simple: the nails of crucified victims were regarded as some of the most powerful charms, or amulets, in the ancient world. Ordinary people prized them very highly, believing that they had healing properties. And apart from their popularity as charms, the crucifixion nails were often reused by the Roman soldiers. So immediately after crucified victims were cut down from their crosses, the nails would be removed from their bodies and pocketed.

No wonder the bones of only one clearly crucified victim have ever been found – not because animals ate the remains off a rubbish tip, but because there is no way for archaeologists to tell if the bones found in tombs were those of crucifixion victims or not. Those tell-tale signs, like nails stuck through bones, are always missing.

So why was the bone of Jehohannan discovered with a nail still through it? Why didn't looters make off with it, or Roman soldiers reuse it? Well, the answer lies in that particular nail. It has a bent tip. When they took his body down from the cross, they must have found they could not prize it out. When Jehohannan was nailed to his cross, this nail must have hit a knot in the wood and bent, fixing it to the bone for good. So the discovery of this bone does not mean that Jesus' body was thrown to the dogs. In fact, there are strong grounds for thinking that Jesus – like all Jews – would have been given a proper burial.

Under Jewish law everyone, even the most despised criminal, had to have a proper burial in order to save the land from being defiled. To that end, there were strict procedures for the disposal of bodies, which had to be laid in tombs by sunset on the day of death. All the evidence suggests that the Romans would have respected local religious customs. The strength of their empire was built on adaptability and tolerance of indigenous beliefs, as long as they didn't contradict the aims and beliefs of the Romans themselves. History records that, more than once, Pontius Pilate himself caved in to Jewish demands.

To expose the corpse of an executed Jew beyond the interval permitted by the Law, and then to allow it to be mutilated by scavengers just outside the city of Jerusalem, was a recipe for a riot. So, what would have happened to Jesus' body? The normal practice would have been to wash, perfume and bind the body so that it wouldn't smell in the heat at the funeral seven days later. This was a laborious procedure which could take up to twenty-four

131

hours. It was governed by religious custom and by a powerful sense of respect for the body.

But if Jesus died in the afternoon, as the gospel accounts suggest, then there would not have been sufficient time to prepare the body that day. The women would be forced to leave the body unwashed in the sealed tomb, then come back another day to finish the job. However, the timing was very unfortunate. According to the gospel accounts, Jesus died on a Friday, in which case the women could not return the following day – Saturday – as that day was the Sabbath. The earliest opportunity for the women to attend to the

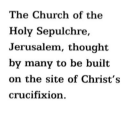

The Church of the Holy Sepulchre, Jerusalem, thought by many to be built on the site of Christ's crucifixion.

body of Jesus was first light Sunday morning, precisely when the gospels say the women did return to the tomb.

So, it is perfectly plausible that Jesus' body was placed in a tomb after his death, and that the women came to it on the third day, just as the gospels describe. But the gospel writers claim much more than that. They suggest that the tomb was empty because a miracle had taken place, because Jesus had risen from the dead. How can that claim be examined?

Well, theologians set about the task in much the same way that we examine any remarkable or contentious event in our own time: by scrutinizing the motives and accounts of eyewitnesses who were there at the right place and time, and the reporters who mediate the eyewitness accounts to us. Did the eyewitnesses or the reporters make the story up? Who can we believe?

FOLLOWING SPREAD:
The shore of the
Sea of Galilee near
Magdala.

What was Sabbath Law?

The Jewish Sabbath – from the Hebrew *shabbat*, meaning 'to cease' – was Saturday, and on that day Jews had a religious duty to rest, pray and abstain from all work. Sabbath law was observed in the time of Jesus, and is still kept by religious Jews across the world today.

The definition of work was broad and strict, and for the women who wanted to honour and prepare Jesus' body for burial, there was no alternative but to wait a day until the Sabbath had passed, then attend to the body on Sunday. Ironically perhaps, Jesus himself upset the religious authorities by questioning the strict observance of the Sabbath when he felt there was a greater need to be served, as in this account from Mark's Gospel:

'He went into the synagogue, and a man with a shrivelled hand was there. Some of them were looking for a reason to accuse Jesus, so they watched him closely to see if he would heal on the Sabbath. Jesus said to the man with the shrivelled hand, "Stand up in front of everyone." Then Jesus asked them, "Which is lawful on the Sabbath: to do good or to do evil, to save life or to kill?" But they remained silent. He looked round at them in anger and, deeply distressed at their stubborn hearts, said to the man, "Stretch out your hand." He stretched it out, and his hand was completely restored.'

MARK 3:1–5

133

CHAPTER FOURTEEN

Did the reporters make it all up?

On 22 November 1963 in Dallas, Texas, President John F Kennedy was assassinated. America was shaken to the core. As the news flashed around the globe, that shock was felt by everyone. Key images from that bright southern day became iconic: the young leader smiling and waving from the back seat of his open-topped car; the distraught widow; the vice-president being sworn in as the new commander-in-chief.

In a modern context, it was a hugely significant event, but not a simple event to understand. Partly because of its importance to the people of America, it is still being fought over more than forty years on. And there are many unanswered questions: did Lee Harvey Oswald act alone in killing the president? Or was there a second assassin standing somewhere nearby on the so-called 'grassy knoll'? Eyewitness accounts and evidence – like the Zapruder home movie of that morning in Dallas – are still pored over in tremendous detail.

Why is the JFK assassination evidence still so controversial? Because what you believe happened in Dallas that day affects your view of America. If you believe Kennedy was the victim of a conspiracy, then you're likely to believe the US is secretive and oppressive, run by organized crime and the CIA. If you believe he was killed by Oswald acting alone, then maybe the US is still the land of the free, and a freak crime like that could happen anywhere. The stakes are high, and that is why the debate continues.

If that is how we struggle to make sense of iconic events in our own lifetime, then perhaps it is not surprising that the evidence for the resurrection of Jesus is still the subject of so much contention and dispute. Of course, the stakes in this debate are far higher. What you believe happened in that tomb on the third day after Jesus was crucified affects your view of Jesus, and your view of the whole history of Christianity.

If you weren't a direct witness to the events in question, then you are reliant on other people who were. Most of us were not standing on the sidewalk of Dealey Plaza when the president's motorcade drove by. And none of us was walking out of an empty tomb in Jerusalem when we met an oddly familiar stranger who called us by name.

So if we can't trust the judgment of our own eyes on these occasions, we have to trust other kinds of authority, namely reporters and eyewitnesses. In the case of JFK, the reporters include the campaigning journalists, film-makers and governmental investigators who gathered every piece of information they could glean about that November day and built an argument with a conclusion. The eyewitnesses are fewer, and a dwindling group as the years pass.

Reporters mediate the eyewitnesses to us. And that raises some very pointed questions. Can we trust the reporters? Are they unbiased? Do we believe the eyewitnesses? Could they be deluded or lying? In the case of the resurrection, we have the eyewitnesses – people like Mary Magdalene and Peter – who claim to have seen Jesus alive after his death. Do we believe them? Could they be mistaken? And then we have the reporters – the gospel writers who pass on the eyewitness accounts. Can we trust them? Are they unbiased?

The assassination of John F Kennedy. The ways in which people view this event are often related to their beliefs about the world in general.

Theologians and historians for generations have wrestled with these questions, and the arguments begin with the reporters: Matthew, Mark, Luke and John. What can we know about their motives, their background? At first glance, the answer seems to be 'very little', as there are precious few glimpses of autobiography in the gospels. All their focus is on Jesus' life and work.

However, by examining the similarities and differences between these four accounts of the same events, and by contrasting the way different events in Jesus' life are reported, scholars have been able to test and explore the evidence of these 'reporters'.

Who were the four evangelists?

Each of the gospels has its own particular emphasis. They are four portraits which, when taken together, build up a picture of Jesus.

Matthew wrote his Gospel between AD 75 and 85, possibly in Antioch. The Gospel does not identify its author, but from the early church it has been attributed to Matthew the apostle and former tax-collector. Much of Matthew's material is almost identical to Mark's and scholars believe he drew on Mark's Gospel as a source for his own. Matthew was a Jewish Christian, writing predominantly for his fellow Jews. In a formal and traditional literary style he focuses on Jesus as the longed-for Jewish Messiah, in fulfilment of Jewish prophecy. In Matthew's portrait, Jesus is a judge, criticizing the Jews for their unfaithfulness to their religion. He is particularly strong in his condemnation of the Pharisees, accusing them of hollow religiosity and hypocrisy. For Matthew, the miracles of Jesus are fulfilments of the Jewish scriptures, and therefore function as evidence for his messianic status.

Mark's Gospel was written between AD 65 and 75. Again, he is not clearly identified in his own text, but there is a strong early tradition that the author is John Mark, a cousin of Paul's companion Barnabas, who was setting down the story of Jesus exactly as he had heard it from the lips of Peter. Presumed to have been written in Rome, Mark's Gospel has a habit of spelling out and explaining Jewish customs, as if to make the details clear for a wide non-Jewish audience. Mark's emphasis is more on the actions than the words of Jesus. In particular, he stresses the healing miracles, as part of an ongoing battle in which Jesus challenges and overcomes evil.

The author of Luke's Gospel is believed to be a doctor who accompanied Paul on his missionary journeys. The precise and detailed descriptions of diseases, and how Jesus healed them, fits with this assumption. Luke writes as an educated man with a wide vocabulary, and is at home with Greek and Jewish culture. He worked with the Gospel of his fellow evangelist

Of course, questioning the gospel writers is a contentious activity, and the contention begins with the very first miracle – the birth of Jesus. According to Christian tradition, Jesus was born to Mary, a woman who had had no prior sexual relationship. An angel appeared to Mary nine months beforehand, announcing that she would give birth to a child. The virgin birth is a remarkable story, and it makes a huge claim. You might expect such an unprecedented and miraculous event to be reported by all four gospel writers, but in fact the story is only reported by Matthew and Luke. It is not part of the accounts set down by Mark and John. Why not?

Mark, and clearly knew it well. Writing between AD 85 and 95, Luke's Gospel is the first half of a two-part Christian history, which continues with the book of Acts. His chief concern is to establish the truth of what happened in the years of Jesus' ministry. His Gospel is full of human compassion, especially for the poor, the sick, women, children and the marginalized. Luke emphasizes that Jesus' miracles are performed by the power of the Holy Spirit, and are signs of the liberation of the people from oppression.

'The beloved disciple' is a term used by John the evangelist to describe his own relationship with Jesus. He makes no mention of the apostle John, and refers to John the Baptist simply as 'John', so some scholars in the past have concluded that he was himself John, son of Zebedee, brother of James, and one of the twelve disciples. This suggested link between John the evangelist and John the son of Zebedee is now seen as more contentious, but its power comes from the unique eyewitness position of John the disciple. He was one of the inner circle of three close disciples who witnesses the transfiguration of Jesus on the mountain top and the raising of Jairus' daughter from the dead. John was also close to Jesus in the garden of Gethsemane in the hours leading up to his arrest, so he had a special insight into the events he is describing. Whether or not its author was John the disciple, the Gospel of John was the last of the four Gospels to be written – dating from around AD 90–110 – and seems to assume that many of the facts of Jesus' life are already known to the reader. From Jesus' many miracles, John selects seven 'signs' that demonstrate most clearly Jesus' identity as the Son of God.

The end of Mark's Gospel and the beginning of Luke's, from the Codex Sinaiticus, middle of fourth century.

Some theologians believe this is a telling inconsistency. To them, it sows a seed of doubt about the authenticity of the virgin birth. If only two of the evangelists report such a big story, then did it really happen? Was Jesus really born of a virgin? Did Matthew or Luke simply make up the miracle as a powerful way of opening their accounts of Jesus' life? Scholars are still divided

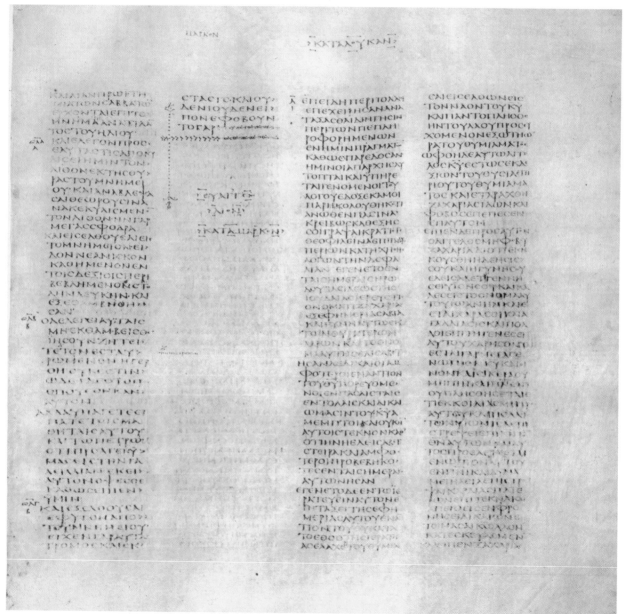

on that issue. For some, it confirms their argument that the gospels are not reliable historical documents. For others, however, Mark and John had sound theological reasons for leaving the birth narrative out of their gospels. It is reasonable to look for principled explanations for why the gospel writers arranged their material differently rather than drawing the conclusion that one or other is necessarily in error.

If the evangelists were primarily in the business of spreading the good news about Jesus, then maybe that took precedence over the business of producing accurate reports. But where does that leave the case for the resurrection? Well, even the most sceptical scholar would admit that the gospel accounts of the resurrection follow a different pattern. Unlike the story of the virgin birth, the resurrection is reported by all four gospel writers. On grounds of consistency, the reporters' accounts of the resurrection cannot be dismissed

Was Jesus born of a virgin?

The virgin birth remains a central pillar of the Christian story, but one that still divides theological opinion. The case against the historical reality of the virgin birth is built on scepticism about supernatural events, but also on the fact that two of the four gospels do not mention it, and it doesn't appear in any of Paul's letters. For some theologians, the virgin birth was a narrative device to begin the story of Jesus with a spectacular intervention by God, to demonstrate from the outset that Jesus was unlike any other man.

The case for belief in the reality of the virgin birth is built on its uniqueness. Scholars still debate whether the concept of a virgin birth was present in Jewish or pagan literature. However, it seems there was no clear precedent or expectation of such a birth in first-century Judaism, so it would not function as a known symbol for a storyteller to use to herald the arrival of a significant person. Both sceptics and believers alike agree that there was something unusual or unconventional about Jesus' birth. His mother was young and, at the time of his conception, unmarried.

At the very least it can be said that Jesus was conceived out of wedlock. Some theologians have argued that it would be difficult for the gospel writers to make up stories of virginal conception while members of Jesus' family were still alive, as Jesus' brother James would have been. In fact, it seems likely that Jesus' family was the source from which the account of Jesus' birth came.

as unreliable. But there's a problem. The evangelists did not write their accounts at the same time.

John wrote his Gospel around AD 90–110 – sixty years after Jesus' death. Matthew and Luke wrote theirs a decade earlier. And Mark wrote his account first – around AD 65–75 – thirty years after Jesus' death. Is it possible that Mark, as the earliest of the reporters, invented the story of the resurrection, and later evangelists copied and embellished his version?

We don't know much about the author of Mark's Gospel. But piecing together clues in his writing, scholars have managed to build up a fragmentary picture of the man. The first discovery was that 'Mark' wrote his Gospel not in the Holy Land, but in the capital of the mighty empire itself – Rome. He must have been under tremendous pressure, hundreds of miles from Galilee and Jerusalem, writing thirty years after Jesus' death, to try to convert as many Romans as possible to the new Christian faith. He was working at a crucial make-or-break moment for the church. It is easy to imagine a strong temptation to exaggerate and embellish the story, maybe even to make a few things up altogether.

It is possible, of course. But to make that case implies other arguments. If Mark invented the whole story of the resurrection, a story so convincing that hundreds of millions of people based their lives on it, then he was nothing short of a master story-maker, a master of fiction. Was Mark capable of such imaginative depth? The textual evidence suggests not.

The first thing a master storyteller would do – if he wanted to convince his audience of the truth of an outlandish claim like the resurrection of the dead – is to build his case on carefully constructed accounts placed in the mouths of rock-solid eyewitnesses. And in first-century Israel that would have meant a *man*, preferably a fine, sane and upstanding member of the community.

Mark even had the ideal candidate – Joseph of Arimathea, the man who donated his tomb to bury Jesus. Joseph was a wealthy Jew and a member of the Sanhedrin. Mark couldn't have asked for a more convincing witness. He was on the scene in the last days of Jesus' life, so even though he was not there on the actual day of the resurrection, it would not be hard to stretch a point and use him as a top-class eyewitness in the story.

Women, on the other hand, were deemed highly unreliable. So much so that under Jewish law they didn't even count as legal witnesses. Women were the very last people a master storyteller would have chosen to use as witnesses. Yet that's precisely what Mark does. The key eyewitnesses to the resurrection are women. It is the women who visit Jesus' tomb on the third day after his death who provide the first-hand accounts. They found the tomb empty, and they met the risen Jesus before anyone else.

But it is not just that Mark uses women as witnesses. One of his star witnesses is Mary Magdalene – according to Luke chapter 8, a woman formerly

Mary Magdalene

She was with Jesus throughout the turbulent last years of his life. She saw him crucified. She was the first to meet him risen from the dead. He chose her as the one to take the news of his resurrection to the other disciples. Her name was Mary. But she was not his virgin mother. Tradition tells us that this Mary was very different, a prostitute forgiven by Jesus, a woman whose name is a symbol of sin and repentance – Mary Magdalene.

As a young woman in a poverty stricken occupied land, it is possible that Mary could have been a prostitute. But scholars now believe it is likely that Mary 'of Magdala' was not a prostitute at all, just an unmarried woman.

She is described in Luke's Gospel as one 'from whom seven demons had gone out', and she has passed into history as a woman healed by Jesus of demon possession. In modern medical terms, it has been suggested that she suffered from epilepsy, or from a psychiatric disorder.

Recent scholarship, informed by the discovery of an ancient document in the Egyptian desert, has begun to re-evaluate the life of Mary Magdalene and her role in the early church. The document, known as the 'Gospel of Mary', seems to portray her as a trusted disciple of Jesus, one of his inner circle.

It challenges the traditional image of Mary Magdalene as a penitent prostitute hanging around the fringes of the Jesus movement. According to Matthew, Mark and Luke's Gospels, Mary is the first to take the news to the disciples. But apart from her crucial role at the end of the gospels, Mary Magdalene is a very minor player in the gospel stories of Jesus.

If she wasn't a prostitute, or an outcast, then why isn't she a key figure in the early church? Why isn't her name uttered in the same breath as Peter or Paul? In the Gospel of Mary, we see her not only as companion and disciple of Jesus, but as teacher and spiritual guide to the other disciples.

In 1969, the Vatican revoked the tag 'penitent' from Mary's Day in the Catholic calendar. Mary was back to being an 'ordinary' saint. The academic debate continues about this remarkable woman, who may have been a founder of the Christian faith.

possessed by demons. No one constructing a false account would dream of using such questionable authorities to convince a first-century audience.

However, if Mark wasn't writing fiction, then different rules apply. As a faithful reporter, you can't pluck your eyewitnesses from the air. Reporters writing about the JFK assassination might have longed for a solid witness who saw Oswald with a smoking gun, but they had to make do with fragmentary accounts from whoever happened to be at the roadside that day.

Most theologians conclude that Mark uses the least impressive witnesses as evidence for the story of the resurrection because they were there at the scene. It's hardly the work of a writer using fiction to win hearts and minds. In fact it suggests Mark was another kind of writer entirely. Not someone who felt free to make things up but rather someone working with memories and eyewitness accounts *handed down* to him – information he simply couldn't tamper with. In other words, Mark's Gospel displays the hallmarks of someone *faithfully* reporting what he'd heard – an extraordinary story about a man who'd been raised from the dead.

So if Mark was using earlier sources, where did they come from? Certainly not from Matthew, Luke or John, who wrote their gospels after Mark.

Early church sources say Mark got the data for his Gospel from someone who knew Jesus intimately, someone who actually claimed to have met the resurrected Jesus just days after the tomb was found empty – the disciple Peter.

But can we believe Peter and the disciples' claims that they'd seen Jesus after he'd been raised from the dead? Even if they weren't lying, could they be deluded? They were the only eyewitnesses, and eyewitnesses are the backbone of any case. Without them, the reporters cannot write a word. To establish the truth, you have to examine the eyewitnesses.

CHAPTER FIFTEEN:

Did the eyewitnesses make it all up?

If Mark based his gospel account of the resurrection on the testimony of the disciple Peter, and if Mark's Gospel was the earliest, then that makes Peter a crucial eyewitness.

Peter was a leading missionary of the early church, travelling extensively throughout the empire, before ending up in Rome. His qualifications as a missionary for Jesus were second to none. He had been one of the twelve disciples, perhaps even Jesus' right-hand man. Peter had been one of the first of Jesus' followers to hear from Mary Magdalene and Mary the mother of James that the tomb had been found empty. The combination of his close proximity to the events in the last week of Jesus' life and his subsequent travel and work as a missionary for the cause make Peter a very plausible source for Mark's story that Jesus had been raised from the dead. But what kind of a man was Peter? And can we trust him?

Peter was a man of conviction, a man who believed with all his heart that Jesus was the Messiah. Why else would he have given his life to the dangerous task of spreading the message of this new movement? But if his expectations of the Messiah were anything like those we see in the Dead Sea Scrolls, then there's a mystery here. Surely the sight of Jesus dying on the cross should have changed his mind?

It is true, of course, that a person with conviction is hard to change, but when faced with overwhelming evidence to the contrary, surely even the most stubborn of people would drop their convictions? Well, in the case of the death of the Messiah, that is clearly not the case. After that ignominious defeat, Peter became more and more convinced that Jesus was God, and that he was alive again. What was the basis for this conviction? One possibility is the one cited in the gospels: that Jesus had indeed been raised from the dead. But there is another theory.

In the early 1950s a group of American scientists claimed they could show why some people refuse to drop their convictions and beliefs, even when the evidence is piled high against them.

The story began in Minnesota, which became the focus of a remarkable anthropological experiment carried out by sociologists at the University of Minnesota. Though not theologians, their work was to have a significant impact on our understanding of those vital early days after the crucifixion, when the Jesus movement hit its lowest ebb.

In an ordinary house in Minnesota, a woman named Marion Keech held some extraordinary beliefs. She was fascinated by the idea of aliens and flying saucers. In fact, she was more than fascinated. In 1954, she began to receive messages which were – she claimed – bulletins from outer space. She carefully wrote down these messages, believing them to be important, and before long she had persuaded other people to join her. This group claimed that their extraterrestrial messages were just a kind of preamble. Mrs Keech, they announced, was on the threshold of receiving a message of vital importance to the whole world.

Marion Keech (real name Dorothy Martin) who claimed to receive bulletins from outer space.

Sure enough, one hot day in August 1954, she began to write down the following message: 'In the midst of this it is to be recorded that a great wave rushes into the Rocky Mountains... In the area of the Mississippi, in the region of Canada, Great Lakes...' The message clearly warned that a massive flood would engulf America on December 21. At first, Mrs Keech told her group to keep the information secret. Only if they kept the secret – and kept their faith in Mrs Keech and her messages – would they be saved. And salvation would come in the shape of a flying saucer.

By September, the level of anticipation in the group was growing. Mrs Keech could no longer keep her extraordinary secret, so she told the local press about the messages, and specifically about the flood warning. The local newspaper carried the following story: 'Prophecy from planet. Clarion call to

146

city: flee that flood. It'll swamp us on December 21, outer space tells suburbanite.'

At this point, the previously secretive group came to the attention of sociologists at the University of Minnesota. The academics were immediately struck by the parallels with the story of the resurrection of Jesus. Here was a leader who – like Jesus two thousand years before – was urging her followers to keep faith with her promise. For the sociologists it was a unique opportunity to see what would happen when the cult members' hopes were dashed – as they surely would be. Would they immediately drop their convictions, overwhelmed by the weight of evidence against them? Or would they doggedly cling on to them? If they did keep the faith, despite the evidence, then that could shed new light on why the disciples refused to drop their convictions. Maybe groups can build a future on a lie? Maybe they can convince themselves?

Peter and the church

Peter is famous as the first among the disciples, the rock on which Jesus founded his church, and the disciple who denied knowledge of Jesus to protect himself when questioned by the authorities following Jesus' arrest.

According to the gospels, his original name was Simon, but the name Peter (from the Greek word for 'rock') was given to him by Jesus, who saw him as a solid foundation on which the future church could be built. When called by Jesus to follow him and become a disciple, Peter was a Galilean fisherman. After the death and resurrection of Jesus, Peter was one of the leaders of the fledgling Jesus movement in Jerusalem.

The Jerusalem church, led by James the brother of Jesus, focused its evangelistic efforts on Jews in the city itself, and taught that Jewish customs such as circumcision and the keeping of the Law should continue after conversion to Christianity. When the apostle Paul began his own mission to the Gentiles, and told them that they need not be circumcised or follow the Law, it was Peter who visited Paul to try to reconcile the two sides.

Very little is known about the later mission of Peter, though he remained a leading figure in the movement as it spread out into the wider Roman empire. He was martyred in Rome, though there is no clear evidence that he served as a bishop of the church there.

A UFO flying over New Mexico in 1957. There is no conventional explanation for the object.

So, a couple of the faculty members decided to infiltrate the cult by posing as new recruits. Once inside, they were party to all discussions and developments. So they joined the other members in ticking off the days on the calendar. According to the extraterrestrial messages received by Mrs Keech, the group would be rescued by flying saucer five days before the colossal flood. All they had to do was to gather in the yard of Mrs Keech's house on December 17.

To the bewilderment of the group – but not the academics – 17 December duly came and went, with no sign of a flying saucer coming to the rescue. Disappointed, but not dejected, the group picked itself up and looked forward

to 21 December when the flood would finally come. Surely the group would be rescued in the nick of time?

On the evening before the promised flood – December 20 – the group gathered in Mrs Keech's living room. She had received a new message that they would be rescued at midnight. As the hands of the clock crept towards the hour in question, the phone rang. It was a local reporter, asking if they had been rescued yet. Mrs Keech remained polite and calm. There was no news yet, she said.

When the apocalyptic hour came and went without incident, the Keech group story slid down the list of priorities for radio, television and newspapers. No longer a macabre 'what if' story, they were painted as a group of deluded eccentrics. The prophetic moment had come and gone. The world had not ended. America was not drowned in a deluge. Marion Keech and her followers had not been rescued by a flying saucer. This was the moment the sociologists had been waiting for. How would the group react to the collapse of all its beliefs and predictions? Surely now, they would drop the whole extraterrestrial story and fade away?

Several hours after the appointed time, the sociologists report that the group was still gathered in Marion Keech's house. The mood was pensive and melancholic. They were trying to make sense of what had happened, or rather what had not happened. As the hours dragged on, some broke down and cried. Almost all lost their composure. They were all visibly shaken. The group – it seemed – was on the verge of collapse.

Then suddenly Marion Keech summoned everyone into her living room, announcing that she had just received a message: 'Not since the beginning of time has there been such a force of good and light as now floods this room, and that which has been loosed within this room now floods the entire earth. Mighty is the word of God – and by his word have ye been saved.'

The message was exactly what the downcast group wanted to hear. They hadn't been deluded all along. The reason there had been no deluge was because of the group itself. These few believers in Minnesota had spread so much light around the world that God had called off the cataclysm. Victory had been snatched from the jaws of defeat. The news was to be made public as a Christmas message to people all over the world.

The academics, still posing as followers of Mrs Keech, were astounded. Instead of abandoning their beliefs under the weight of contrary evidence, this dejected and disillusioned group simply adjusted their beliefs to suit the circumstances. Effectively, Mrs Keech's latest message gave them a new set of beliefs. At once, they began to spread the good news to newspapers, radio and television, hoping to win new converts to their cause. And in the meantime, Mrs Keech continued to receive messages from extraterrestrials. Supported and comforted by each other at the crucial moment when it all went wrong for them, Marion Keech and her group was now galvanized with renewed fire and optimism. The sociologists were cock-a-hoop, and no wonder. The parallels with the story of Jesus' disciples were inescapable.

When that band of Jewish rebels saw their charismatic leader nailed to a cross and left to die, they must have been demoralized and distraught. This was the man they believed would be the saviour of Israel. But like Marion Keech and her followers, they did not abandon the faith. Instead, they spread the word of a remarkable new belief – that Jesus had come back from death, and they had met him.

As with Marion Keech, one extraordinary belief had been replaced by another. In both cases, the new conviction provided a way out of the crushing disappointment. And crucially, in both cases the followers spread the good news to the world. It was a conviction that gave them strength and a new sense of purpose.

The parallels between the experiences of this Minnesota UFO cult group and those of Jesus' disciples have become a classic case study. For many people, the comparison seems, at first glance, to illustrate why the disciples came to believe in the resurrection of Jesus. Perhaps they – and the disciples of Marion Keech – needed a turnaround so desperately that they created one. Whether that creation was conscious or unconscious, it seems to say more about the psychological state of that particular group than about any objective historical event.

But there is twist in the tale of Marion Keech and her UFO group. For all the apparent parallels, their story and the story of Jesus' disciples differ in one vital respect. The UFO group held together for barely a few months. After the

The persecution of the first Christians

From the outset, Jesus made it clear that following him would not be easy. In Matthew's Gospel he is quoted warning his disciples that he came 'not to bring peace, but a sword'. Apart from the obvious ructions caused by becoming a member of a radical cult attached to an ancient and established religion, the risks taken by disciples of Jesus to follow him could lead to the loss of family, home, livelihood and social standing.

In Paul's letters, the persecution of the early church is given voice by a man who had worked as a persecutor. In his previous life as Saul, he had worked for the Jewish authorities to stamp out seditious and heretical movements, including the early Jesus movement. For Paul, the turning point was in an encounter with the risen Christ on the road to Damascus, when he was en route to track down a burgeoning group of Christians in that city.

The Emperor Commodus dressed as Hercules. Early Christians refused to participate in emperor worship.

The Roman attitude to rival religions within its empire was generally pretty tolerant. Roman paganism allowed for a range of gods being worshipped alongside each other, as well as a range of local and regional deities picked up as the empire spread. But there were conditions imposed on citizens of the empire, to maintain this religious tolerance. Whatever the range of gods being worshipped in a place, the Roman emperor must be among them, and when push came to shove the emperor was the chief god.

The refusal of the early Christians to participate in emperor worship – which they regarded as idolatrous – combined with their insistence that the Christian God was the one true and universal god, put them beyond the pale as far as the Romans were concerned.

151

initial excitement, members began to disperse, falling away and losing contact with each other, until finally the group ceased to exist altogether.

The Jesus movement was quite different. His followers did not just stay together for a few months. They held together for years – in Jerusalem and Galilee – in the face of fierce persecution. Then Peter and the other disciples began to travel around the Roman empire converting people to the new faith.

Unlike the members of the Minnesota UFO cult, the early Christians were prepared to put their lives on the line for their cause. A long list of Jesus' followers were killed as martyrs for their faith. Peter himself – who in the last weeks of Jesus' earthly life had denied knowing him, for fear of invoking the wrath of the authorities – went on to risk everything to spread the Christian message, and was finally crucified upside-down in Rome.

Peter's conviction that Jesus had been raised from the dead had a powerful impact on his own life, but it also left a lasting legacy. Thirty years after Peter's death, the movement was spreading like wildfire through the Roman empire. And two thousand years on, it is the world's largest religion. The parallels with Marion Keech's group now seem more tenuous. Her conviction that their tiny group had saved the world lasted a few months and left no legacy except an academic case study. Something far more real, far more powerful, must have convinced Peter that Jesus' tomb was empty on the third day after his death.

To achieve what the early Christians did, and to make such sacrifices, it is not enough just to believe that your master might have come back to life. Of course, that would be remarkable, but to put your life on the line you would need a clear sense of the implications of the resurrection. The only way to make sense of Christian history is to examine what this greatest of miracles meant to those who witnessed and believed in it.

CHAPTER SIXTEEN

Did Jesus know he would be resurrected?

The conventional wisdom is that the disciples were genuinely astonished by the empty tomb and the appearances of Jesus. But in fact there were clues in a number of Jesus' miracles, clues that the disciples may well have picked up on.

Just days before entering Jerusalem for the last time, Jesus went to a village called Bethany. He had received news that a friend of his had died. In John's gospel account, what Jesus does in Bethany is beautiful and powerfully symbolic.

'On his arrival, Jesus found that Lazarus had already been in the tomb for four days. Bethany was less than two miles from Jerusalem, and many Jews had come to Martha and Mary to comfort them in the loss of their brother.

Bethany, the site of one of Jesus' most powerful miracles.

When Martha heard that Jesus was coming, she went out to meet him, but Mary stayed at home. "Lord," Martha said to Jesus, "if you had been here, my brother would not have died. But I know that even now God will give you whatever you ask." Jesus said to her, "Your brother will rise again." Martha answered, "I know he will rise again in the resurrection at the last day." Jesus said to her, "I am the resurrection and the life. He who believes in me will live, even though he dies; and whoever lives and believes in me will never die. Do

you believe this?" "Yes Lord," she told him, "I believe that you are the Christ, the Son of God, who was to come into the world." And after she had said this, she went back and called her sister Mary aside. "The teacher is here," she said, "and is asking for you." When Mary heard this, she got up quickly and went to him.

Now Jesus had not yet entered the village, but was still at the place where Martha had met him. When the Jews who had been with Mary in the house, comforting her, noticed how quickly she got up and went out, they followed her, supposing she was going to the tomb to mourn there.

When Mary reached the place where Jesus was and saw him, she fell at his feet and said, "Lord, if you had been here, my brother would not have died." When Jesus saw her weeping, and the Jews who had come along with her also weeping, he was deeply moved in spirit and troubled. "Where have you laid him?" he asked. "Come and see Lord," they replied. Jesus wept. Then the Jews said, "See how he loved him!" But some of them said, "Could not he who opened the eyes of the blind man have kept this man from dying?"

Jesus, once more deeply moved, came to the tomb. It was a cave with a stone laid across the entrance. "Take away the stone," he said. "But Lord," said Martha, the sister of the dead man, "by this time there is a bad odour, for he has been there four days." Then Jesus said, "Did I not tell you that if you believed, you would see the glory of God?" So they took away the stone.

Then Jesus looked up and said, "Father, I thank you that you have heard me. I knew that you always hear me, but I said this for the benefit of the people standing here, that they may believe that you sent me." When he had said this, Jesus called in a loud voice, "Lazarus, come out!" The dead man came out, his hands and feet wrapped with strips of linen, and a cloth around his face. Jesus said to them, "Take off the grave clothes and let him go."

JOHN 11:17–44

To the Jews of the first century, bringing a dead person back to life was not unprecedented. According to the Jewish scriptures, Elijah had prayed to God, and brought a widow's son back to life. What was different here in Bethany was the manner of the resuscitation.

Prophets like Elijah had to cry out to God, begging him to revive the widow's boy. And that's because in Jewish belief only God could raise dead people back to life. But when *Jesus* brings people back to life, it is quite different. 'Lazarus, come out!' is the command that brings the man back from death, and those words are uttered directly by Jesus to Lazarus. The miracle takes place by the power of Jesus' own words.

The symbolic message is clear. Jesus himself has power over life and death. That makes him greater than a prophet or a miracle worker. Jesus was acting as God.

And this becomes even clearer when Jesus himself dies, because there were tell-tale differences between the raising of Lazarus and that of Jesus. Lazarus comes out of his tomb bound up in linen, showing that he has risen by another's power. Jesus has to instruct the man's sisters to free him from his bindings. When Jesus is raised from the dead, he leaves his grave clothes behind, because he has risen by his *own* power.

In the early days of the church, the disciples must have looked back on Jesus' life – and especially on miracles like the raising of Lazarus – in the light

'Resurrection' from John Donne's *Holy Sonnets*

Moist with one drop of thy blood, my dry soul
Shall (though she now be in extreme degree
Too stony hard, and yet too fleshly,) be
Freed by that drop, from being starved, hard, or foul,
And life, by this death abled, shall control
Death, whom they death slew; nor shall to me
Fear of first or last death, bring misery,
If in thy little book my name thou enrol,
Flesh in that long sleep is not putrefied,
But made that there, of which, and for which 'twas;
Nor can by other means be glorified.
May then sin's sleep, and death's soon from me pass,
That waked from both, I again risen may
Salute the last, and everlasting day.

of his death and resurrection. If Jesus *was* God, then why *wouldn't* he come back from the dead? With hindsight, it may have seemed almost inevitable.

It seems likely that a number of factors combined to convince the disciples of the reality of the resurrection. It wasn't the empty tomb alone. It wasn't even the appearances of Jesus after his death. It was a combination of remarkable events, including miracles like the raising of Lazarus, which only God could have made happen.

And there was one more factor, perhaps the most important of all. Although Lazarus was brought back to life, he would in due course die again.

The resurrection in the gospels

Accounts of the resurrection are given in Matthew's Gospel in chapter 28, Mark's Gospel in chapter 16, Luke's Gospel in chapter 24 and John's Gospel in chapters 20 and 21.

All four gospels are clear that the resurrection was a real event, and a crucial turning point in history, but they differ on many of the details. When the women enter the tomb and find the body of Jesus gone, Mark describes 'a young man dressed in a white robe sitting on the right side'. The women are shocked to see this figure, but he tells them: 'Don't be alarmed. You are looking for Jesus the Nazarene, who was crucified. He has risen! He is not here. See the place where they laid him. But go, tell his disciples and Peter, "He is going ahead of you into Galilee. There you will see him, just as he told you."' However, in Matthew's account, the young man in a white robe is an angel, and in Luke's account there are two angels.

Mark's Gospel ends at chapter 16 verse 8, before any of the resurrection appearances described by the other gospels. In Matthew, there is an elaborate subplot to the disciples' encounters with the risen Christ. This involves some Roman guards who were posted by Pilate to guard the mouth of the tomb in case any of Jesus' followers tried to steal his body. When an angel of the Lord came down and rolled the stone away from Jesus' tomb, those guards were shocked to the core. They went into the city and reported to the chief priests all that they had seen. According to Matthew's account, the soldiers were paid a large sum of money to say that Jesus' disciples came during the night and stole him away while the guards slept. Neither Mark, Luke nor John carries this subplot of the soldiers.

The famous encounter of two of Jesus' disciples with a stranger on the road to Emmaus – perhaps the best known of the so-called 'resurrection appearances' – is both touching and poetic, as they walk and discuss the recent death of their great master, unaware that the man beside them is the risen Jesus. But the Emmaus story is only told in Luke's Gospel.

John alone tells the story of 'doubting' Thomas, the disciple who will not believe that he has met the risen Jesus until he has literally seen and touched the wounds, testing the proof for himself.

After the resurrection, Matthew and Mark have Jesus appearing in his home territory of Galilee, but Luke places him in Jerusalem. John includes post-resurrection accounts from both Galilee and Jerusalem.

Locating the key miracles

The virgin birth of Jesus to Mary
Matthew 1:18–25
Luke 1:26–38

The baptism of Jesus in the river Jordan by John the Baptist
Matthew 3:13–17
Mark 1:9–11
Luke 3:21–22

The feeding of the five thousand, or the miracle of the loaves and fishes
Matthew 14:13–21
Mark 6:35–44
Luke 9:10–17
John 6:1–15

The raising of Lazarus from the dead
John 11:1–44

Jesus walks on the Sea of Galilee
Matthew 14:22–33
Mark 6:45–52
John 6:19–21

Jesus calms the storm
Matthew 8:23–27
Mark 4:35–41
Luke 8:22–25

Jesus casts out the demons – Legion – from possessed man at Gerasa.
Mark 5:1–15
Luke 8:26–33

The turning of water into wine at the wedding at Cana
John 2:1–11

The healing of Syro-Phoenician woman's daughter
Matthew 15:21–28
Mark 7:24–30

The raising from the dead of the widow's son at Nain
Luke 7:11–17

The transfiguration of Jesus
Matthew 17:1–8
Mark 9:2–8
Luke 9:28–36

The healing of the paralyzed man at Capernaum
Matthew 9:2–8
Mark 2:1–12
Luke 5:17–26

The healing of the blind man at Bethsaida
Mark 8:22–26

The resurrection of Jesus
Matthew 28
Mark 16
Luke 24
John 20–21

His was not a resurrection but a resuscitation. The disciples believed that Jesus had been resurrected – to eternal life and an altogether different mode of existence.

Everlasting life has been a dream since the beginning of time. Even today, the newspapers run stories about scientific breakthroughs promising endless life, or endless youth, for all.

If part of the message of Jesus' miracles was that Jesus was God himself, then he could do anything. Perhaps that helps to explain why the disciples came to believe that resurrection was available to anybody who had faith in him. And it was this conviction more than any other that drove those early Christians out into the Roman empire and the world beyond, to pass on the story of a miracle worker from Galilee.

The Christian church today

At the turn of the twenty-first century, Christianity is the most popular religion in the world, with well over two billion followers.

Christianity has spread to all corners of the globe and taken on many different forms in the process. The Roman Catholic Church is the oldest institution in the western world, and the largest Christian denomination. Its centre is in Rome, the home of the pope and the community of theologians and the religious who make up Vatican City. Roman Catholics believe that the pope is the successor to Peter, the disciple of Jesus, who was the first bishop of Rome.

The Eastern Orthodox Church is widespread across central and eastern Europe, and in the former Soviet Union. This self-governing body of Christians believes it is adhering to a pure and unbroken line from the first days of the apostles and the disciples of Jesus.

The Anglican Church is an international communion, centred on Britain and headed by the archbishop of Canterbury.

The many Protestant denominations include Baptists – the fifth largest Christian church in the world – Methodists, Quakers and Pentecostals.

ACKNOWLEDGMENTS

Picture research by Zooid Pictures Limited

2/3 David Alexander; 3 (inset) Tim Macmillan/Time Slice; 8 Christie's Images/Corbis UK Ltd; 9 Michael Nicholson/Corbis UK Ltd; 12/13 Tim Macmillan/Time Slice; 15 Gianni Dagli Orti/Corbis UK Ltd; 18/19 Hanan Isachar; 20 David Townsend/Lion Hudson; 22 www.BibleLandPictures.com/Zev Radovan, Jerusalem; 25 Mimmo Jodice/Corbis UK Ltd; 26 Derek West; 28/29 Archivo Iconografico, S.A./Corbis UK Ltd; 32 David Townsend/Lion Hudson; 34/35 Tim Macmillan/Time Slice; 36 Tim Macmillan/Time Slice; 37 David Townsend/Lion Hudson; 38 Photri/Robert Harding Picture Library; 38/39 David Alexander; 40/41 David Alexander; 44/45 Hanan Isachar; 49 Jonathan Adams; 50 Milner Moshe/Sygma/Corbis UK Ltd; 51 David Townsend/Lion Hudson; 52 Tim Macmillan/Time Slice; 53 David Alexander; 54 Derek West; 54 (inset) David Townsend/Lion Hudson; 56 David Townsend/Lion Hudson; 58 David Townsend/Lion Hudson; 60/61 Tim Macmillan/Time Slice; 62 www.BibleLandPictures.com/Zev Radovan, Jerusalem; 64 Bridgeman Art Library; 66/67 Tim Macmillan/Time Slice; 68 Tim Macmillan/Time Slice; 69 David Alexander; 70/71 David Townsend/Lion Hudson; 75 David Townsend/Lion Hudson; 79 BBC; 80/81 Tim Macmillan/Time Slice; 82/83 David Alexander; 86 Jean-Louis Nou/AKG - Images; 88/89 Tim Macmillan/Time Slice; 92/93 Hanan Isachar; 95 David Alexander; 96/97 Tim Macmillan/Time Slice; 99 Nik Wheeler/Corbis UK Ltd; 103 BBC; 109 BBC; 110 BBC; 112/113 BBC; 114/115 Hanan Isachar; 117 BBC; 118 Richard T. Nowitz/Corbis UK Ltd; 119 Tim Macmillan/Time Slice; 125 Derek West; 126 Chester Beatty Library; 127 Sipa Press/Rex Features; 129 David Townsend/Lion Hudson; 130 Andre Brutmann/Rex Features; 132 David Alexander; 134/135 Hanan Isachar; 137 CPL/Everett/Rex Features; 140 British Library; 146 STF/CEK/AP/Empics; 148/149 Bettmann/Corbis UK Ltd; 151 Araldo de Luca/Corbis UK Ltd; 153 David Alexander; 156/157 BBC